GOD

STILL WORKS

Miracles

S. YVONNE HALL

WESTBOW
PRESS®
A DIVISION OF THOMAS NELSON
& ZONDERVAN

WestBow Press books may be ordered through booksellers or by contacting:

WestBow Press
A Division of Thomas Nelson & Zondervan
1663 Liberty Drive
Bloomington, IN 47403
www.westbowpress.com
844-714-3454

ISBN: 978-1-6642-0617-5 (sc)
ISBN: 978-1-6642-0618-2 (e)

Print information available on the last page.

WestBow Press rev. date: 10/19/2020

DEDICATION

This book is dedicated to six miracles in my life—my children Wanda, Darren, Michele, Bethany, Courtland, Jr., and Jason.

My being called into ministry while they were still young children contributed to a slightly different way of life for them, which could have turned out differently. But thanks be to God and their late father, Courtland, Sr., they have successfully matured, and are now adults of whom I am extremely proud. They are loving, kind, respectful, supportive, and I am so happy to be their mother.

CONTENTS

INTRODUCTION

God moves in mysterious ways, and
<u>M</u>ysterious <u>I</u>ntervention <u>R</u>egulates <u>A</u>nd <u>C</u>hanges <u>L</u>ives <u>E</u>xtraordinarily.

Miracles are not a thing of the past, nor are they just events that happened back in the "Bible days," and this writing is intended to remind readers that events that have happened before can happen today, if it's the will of God.

The dictionary defines a miracle as "an event or effect in the physical world that deviates from known laws of nature or transcends our knowledge of these laws."[1] A miracle can also be defined this way: "A work wrought by a divine power for a divine purpose by means that are beyond the reach of man."[2] Thus, this takes the miracle out of the realm of the natural and elevates it to the supernatural. It gives us to understand that man may work some magic; he may do some sleight of hand, but he does not work miracles. A work that is wrought by a divine power means that it is from God, and even today, God is still working His divine power in the lives of His people.

Some people whom doctors have diagnosed with a terminal illness and for whom they have given up hope, have survived and returned to living a normal life. Some people who have been in horrific automobile accidents have been able to somehow crawl out of the mangled vehicle and walk away unscathed, when one might have assumed that there were no survivors.

During my former employment as a Nurses' Aide in Connecticut at a hospital emergency room (1977-1981), I saw an 18-year-old young woman who had been to her doctor's office for her pre-college check-up. Something happened at the office which was of concern to her doctor, and he sent her, by ambulance, to the emergency room. Once in the emergency room, her condition seemed to worsen and a "code blue" was called (signaling the need for immediate emergency treatment from the emergency team). Being just an aide, I wasn't told her diagnosis; however, by the time I left work at 3:30 p.m., she had been intubated, was on her way to the I.C.U., and her prognosis was not good. The unofficial word was that "she probably wouldn't make it through the night." When I went back to work at 7:00 a.m. the next morning, fearfully (afraid of what the answer might be), I immediately began asking if anyone knew the condition of the young woman who had been brought in the day before. It seemed that everyone knew who I was talking about, and the answer I received was that she was doing exceptionally well. She was sitting up, drinking orange juice, and was expected to be moved from the I.C.U. later in the morning. Not merely "good luck," not "coincidence," not "happenstance," not "a mistake," not the emergency team of doctors, nurses, and technicians, by themselves (remember, they had done all they could do), but this was *"A work wrought by a divine power for a divine purpose by means that are beyond the reach of man."*[3] A miracle!

I am thoroughly convinced, and I believe that God still works miracles today. Births of babies are miracles. When the sperm of a man is united with the egg of a woman, and nine months later a baby (or perhaps two, three or more babies) is born having the looks and characteristics of both mother and father, that's miraculous. When seeds are planted in the ground, covered over and watered, and a few weeks later, either food or flowers are produced, that's miraculous. True—these are miracles of nature and human reproduction that occur daily and as such, they have come to be expected and are accepted as commonplace; however, God is not commonplace. God is not limited to the natural, but He is supernatural. God is not ordinary, but extraordinary, and whatever God has done before, He can do again, if He so chooses.

This book of sermons proclaiming the good news of some of the miracles Jesus performed when He was on earth is also intended to inspire and encourage readers that this power is still at work today. As you read these accounts, however, three important factors should be taken into consideration. First, it must be recognized and understood that there is no specific formula, pattern, or ritual that will guarantee the working of a miracle. God works in mysterious ways according to His will and His providence. Secondly, and of utmost importance, allow the Miracle-Worker to be the focus of your faith rather than the working of the miracle. And thirdly, as shown in the last chapter, God may not always perform a miracle as might be expected, nevertheless, there is a miracle in God's grace which is sufficient to sustain in whatever situation is encountered.

GOD STILL WORKS MIRACLES

John 2:1-11 (NKJV)

¹ On the third day there was a wedding in Cana of Galilee, and the mother of Jesus was there. ² Now both Jesus and His disciples were invited to the wedding. ³ And when they ran out of wine, the mother of Jesus said to Him, "They have no wine." ⁴ Jesus said to her, "Woman, what does your concern have to do with Me? My hour has not yet come." ⁵ His mother said to the servants, "Whatever He says to you, do it." ⁶ Now there were set there six water pots of stone, according to the manner of purification of the Jews, containing twenty or thirty gallons apiece. ⁷ Jesus said to them, "Fill the water pots with water." And they filled them up to the brim. ⁸ And He said to them, "Draw some out now, and take it to the master of the feast." And they took it. ⁹ When the master of the feast had tasted the water that was made wine, and did not know where it came from (but the servants who had drawn the water knew), the master of the feast called the bridegroom. ¹⁰ And he said to him, "Every man at the beginning sets out the good wine, and when the guests have well drunk, then the inferior. You have kept the good wine until now!" ¹¹ This beginning of signs Jesus did in Cana of Galilee and manifested His glory; and His disciples believed in Him.

Jesus' act of turning water into wine at the Wedding Feast of Cana was the occasion of the first recorded miracle that Jesus performed. I want to suggest that there are some interesting factors in the story about this miracle that present themselves as obstacles to our being the beneficiaries of miracles today. But before we explore those factors, let's clearly understand what a miracle is.

The dictionary defines a miracle as "an event or effect in the physical world that deviates from known laws of nature or transcends our knowledge of these laws."[4] A miracle can also be defined this way: "A work wrought by a divine power for a divine purpose by means that are beyond the reach of man." (Dr. McCosh)[5] Thus, this takes the miracle out of the realm of the natural and elevates it to the supernatural. It gives us to understand that man may work some magic; he may do some sleight of hand, but he does not work miracles. A work that is wrought by a divine power means that it is from God.

As we look at the text and the miracle that was performed there in light of the definition, we can readily understand that "turning water into wine" was indeed a work wrought by a divine power, for while Jesus was at the wedding in the flesh–in his humanity—we know that he was not only human, but he was also divine by virtue of his being the son of the living God.

The miracle at Cana was a manifestation of Jesus' glory which quickened and strengthened his disciples' faith in him. And as modern-day followers of Christ, despite ourselves, Jesus still works a miracle every now and then to quicken and strengthen our faith. There are times when the adversities and the vicissitudes of life tend to get us down; times when our faith becomes weak; times when even in our profession of belief, we sometimes demonstrate an expression of doubt and fear; times when the money gets funny and we find ourselves wondering how we're going to meet our financial obligations; times when it seems like there is no answer or solution for some difficult situation or problem. Then suddenly, seemingly out of nowhere, the bill gets paid, the problem is resolved, the healing comes, unexpected blessings appear that are beyond the reach of humanity, and we know that we can run on a little while longer.

Unfortunately, however, when these events occur in some people's lives, they don't want to call it a miracle. They want to say, "it's just a coincidence." They don't want to call it a miraculous blessing; they want to call it "good luck," but I submit that when these prayed for, but unexpected blessings come our way, we need to call them exactly what they are and give God the praise for the great things He and only He (not coincidence, not luck), has done. We need to realize that these are works wrought by a divine power for a divine purpose by means beyond the reach of coincidence or luck. We need to realize that Jesus is manifesting his glory so that our faith in him will be strengthened, and like the disciples, we will believe in His power and know without a shadow of a doubt that with Him, all things are possible.

Notice, if you will, that I said, "...with God, all things **ARE** possible" *(Matthew 19:26),* indicating present tense—right now, right here in in the present. Some people want to relegate miracles to only biblical history. They're willing to accept what they have read in the Bible, but they doubt that there's any real relevance for them today. Please, don't be fooled; don't misunderstand; don't continue to labor under these illusions. Know that God is a relevant, on-time God. God is a "right here" and a "right now" God. The God who was, still is. The God who was back there, back then, is right here, right now. The God who was before time, is now in time and is always on time. The Bible says that He is "...a very present help in the time of trouble."*(Psalm 46:1)* Songwriters have agreed with the Word of God when they wrote: "It is no secret what God can do, what he's done for others, He will do for you."[6]

Have you any rivers that seem to be uncrossable? Just as He parted the waters of the Red Sea for the Children of Israel *(Exodus 14:21-29)*, so He'll part waters of trouble for you. Do some circumstances in your life have you trapped in what seems like a fiery furnace? Just as He delivered Shadrach, Meshack and Abednego *(Daniel 3:19-25)*, so He will deliver you. King Nebuchadnezzar asked the question: "Did we not cast three men bound into the midst of the fire? *(Daniel 3:24)* His counselors answered: "True, O King." The King answered: "Look I see four men loose, walking in the midst of the fire; and they are not hurt, and the form of the fourth is like the Son of God." *(Daniel 3:25)* The fourth man was the Son of God, taking the heat out of the flames. He's still the Son of God, today, still willing to be in the furnace with us when we need Him; still willing to walk through the flames with us, still able to take the heat out of the flames and ready to bring deliverance just as he did for the Hebrew Boys.

God still works miracles, but sometimes we are unable to experience these miracles because we have and demonstrate some behaviors that keep us from receiving our miracle. One such behavior is a **LACK OF FELLOWSHIP** with the Miracle-Worker.

The Bible says that Jesus and his disciples were invited to the wedding *(John 2:2).* In other words, the people had invited Jesus in and began to fellowship with Him, and this invitation was extended before the wine ran out. Some of us don't invite Jesus in until after the wine runs out. We don't invite him in to celebrate the joy of life; we don't invite him in for a season of praise and worship and thanksgiving; we don't invite him in for a time of fellowship and friendship. As long as everything seems to be okay in our lives, as long as the marital road is smooth, and the children are behaving themselves; as long as there's plenty of food on the table and the bills are getting paid on time; as long as the job is secure and we have the use and activity of all of our limbs and our faculties, we may hear that Jesus is in town, but as long as everything is everything in our little corner of the world, some of us do not take the time to extend an invitation for Jesus to come on over and fellowship with us and to celebrate and be thankful for those good times.

However, when things begin to turn sour; when economic recession happens and there's talk of laying off thousands of state workers and other employers laying off employees; when the national budget can't seem to be balanced; when bad things begin to happen to good people, then the invitation goes out, but it's not an invitation to fellowship, but rather an invitation to "fix-it-ship." "Lord, please come in and fix my job situation." "Lord, please come in and fix my body." "Lord, please come in and fix my finances." "Lord, please come in and fix this economy." "Lord, please come in and fix minds and hearts." "Lord please come in and fix it up for us, Fix it! Fix it! Fix it! Kiss the boo boo and make it better…"

In the text, however, Jesus had been invited to come into the wedding celebration prior to the problem. He was invited in to fellowship and to be a part of the happy time that was going on, and when the wine ran out, He was already there. They had already established fellowship. And so, it should be with us. Believe it or not, fellowship with Jesus in the good times will help carry us through the bad times. Fellowship with Jesus in sunshine will sustain us in the time of storm. Fellowship with Jesus in the time of peace will guard our hearts and our minds in the time of confusion. Fellowship with Jesus in the time of prosperity will help us to get through times of poverty. When the invitation to "come in" has already been extended and fellowship has already been established as the result of an on-going relationship, then when trouble comes, when the storms rage, when there's a need for a miracle, He's already there. We don't have to go looking for Him. We don't have to go in search of Him; all we need to do is say "Father!" Because we belong to Him and He belongs to us, we can say "Father!" Because of our constant fellowship we can say "Father!" Because of the personal nature of our relationship we can even get personal and say "My Father" I stretch my hands to Thee, no other help I know. And not only can we cry out to Him, but we can expect to receive an answer from Him. We can even expect a miracle from Him. There's no magic formula–just a matter of fellowship. We can most certainly remove one obstacle to our reception of a miracle by inviting Jesus in and establishing fellowship before we get into trouble; before the praise becomes a plea for help; before the feast turns into famine; before the much becomes meager. In other words, we must invite Jesus in and establish fellowship with Him **before** the wine runs out.

The text goes on to say that "…when they ran out of wine, the mother of Jesus said to Him, "they have no wine." *(John 2:3)* This seems to indicate that she was expecting Him to do something about the situation. "Jesus said to her "Woman, what does your concern have to do with me? My hour has not yet come." *(John 2:4)*

In the early days of my preaching ministry, when reading this passage, it often disturbed me. With my perception of Jesus as a kind, compassionate and loving person, this statement sounded strange to me. It not only sounded strange, but it sounded harsh: *"Woman, what does your concern have to do with thee?"(John 2:4)* And then with my childhood upbringing ringing in my ears which taught complete respect for one's parents, combined with the fifth commandment which says "Honor your father and your mother…" *(Exodus 20:12)*, this statement of Jesus also sounded disrespectful. However, I did some study into the background of this text, and that study shed some light on the subject. First, Jesus' address of His mother as "woman" was not uncommon for that time and that culture.[7] I think it was the present-day connotation of the term "woman" that caused the difficulty for me. Oftentimes, nowadays, we have a way of saying "woman" that sounds harsh and disrespectful. But the Holy Spirit brought to my remembrance that even from the cross, Jesus addressed His mother in the same manner when he said: "Woman, behold your son" *(John 19:26)*, and in that context, by no stretch of the imagination did it carry any sign or sound of harshness or disrespect.

Secondly, I realized that something which had happened forty days earlier made a difference in their former "Mother and Son" relationship. Forty days prior, Jesus had been anointed with the Holy Spirit and had received power to undertake the special work which His Father had given Him to do and now that He had entered into public ministry, everything (including family relationships) had to take second place. In other words, the underlying message for Mary was that she didn't have to worry about this situation. It would be taken care of at the appointed time. It's just as crucial for us to realize that just as Jesus' relationship with His Father was of primary importance, so our relationship with God, the Father must be of primary importance in our lives as well. Once we make the commitment to follow Jesus, then everything else becomes secondary. The Bible says: "He who loves father or mother more than me is not worthy of Me. And he who loves son or daughter more than Me is not worthy of Me." (*Matthew 10:37*). And the next words that Jesus said: "My hour is not yet come," (*John 2:4*) meant that this was not the time for Him to perform the action that Mary wanted for the purpose that she wanted. This was not in keeping with His divine purpose.

And so, it is with us sometimes. The things we want and the purpose for which we want them are not always in keeping with God's plan for us or are not always according to His timetable, and many times our **LACK OF PATIENCE**, our unwillingness to wait on God causes us to miss out on our miracle. Somehow, we've got to learn how to wait on God; wait on His timing; wait until His hour has come to work on our behalf.

This is a big problem in this microwave age—in our secular society in which we hardly have to wait for anything anymore. Because of the institution of the "Instant This" and the "Rapid That," we've become an impatient people and we want everything yesterday. We sometimes use, misuse, and abuse other people in our quest for "instant success." There are certain ways and means in which we try to attain "instant wealth" and "instant gratification." I want to remind us that in some cases, things that come instantly are only temporary. In other words, things that sometimes come quickly, go just as quickly. On the other hand, things that are lasting and worth having are worth waiting for, and we need to learn to wait. The Psalmist, David said: *"Wait on the Lord; Be of good courage and He shall strengthen your heart..."* (*Psalm 27:14*). The Prophet, Isaiah put it this way:

"...those who wait on the Lord shall renew their strength; They shall mount up with wings like eagles, They shall run and not be weary, They shall walk and not faint." (Isaiah 40:31) God is still working miracles, and if we have patience and wait on Him, there is a miracle with our name on it. He may move our mountain (and that would be a miracle), but even if He doesn't, He'll give us the strength to climb the mountain. He may remove the stumbling block that's in our way (and that would be a miracle), but if He doesn't, He'll turn that stumbling block into a steppingstone that will bring us up to another level. Or He might simply lead us safely around the mountain, the stumbling block and any other obstacles. No matter how it's done, He's working on our behalf, We must keep in mind that we *"just can't hurry God, we've just got to wait; we've got to trust Him and give Him time, no matter how long it takes. He's a God that we can't hurry, He'll be there we don't have to worry; He may not come when we want Him, but He's right on time."*[8]

Finally, after Jesus had told Mary that His hour had not yet come, she went to the servants and said to them, "whatever He says to you, do it." *(John 2:5)* In other words, obey Him. This third point has to do with Mary's trust and faith in her son. In spite of His response to her, Mary was not discouraged; she was not daunted; she was not rebuffed; she was not put off for she was confident that now that the situation had been given to Him that He would take care of it. Although she may not have fully understood His response, she had faith enough to trust Him. She didn't know what He would do, but she knew He would do something, and it would be the right thing.

Not only is our hindrance to receiving our miracle caused by a lack of obedience, and a lack of patience, but sometimes, we demonstrate a **LACK OF TRUST** which also hinders our receiving our miracle. A lack of (or an absence of) trust is an indication of the presence of doubt, and James says that when one asks, "let him ask in faith, with no doubting, for he who doubts is like a wave of the sea driven and tossed by the wind. For let not that man suppose that he will receive anything from the Lord; *he is* a double-minded man, unstable in all his ways."*(James 1:6-8)* So, we must learn to trustingly commit our situations to Jesus, in spite of the circumstances. Despite how situations may look, despite how they may feel, despite what seems impossible to us based on our logic, education, and intelligence, we need to put all of that aside, pay attention to the words of the writer of Proverbs and "Trust in the LORD with all your heart, And lean not on your own understanding; In all your ways acknowledge Him, And He shall direct your paths". *(Proverbs 3:5,6)*

Do you know what Trust is? Trust <u>is an assured reliance on the character, ability, strength, and truth of someone or something</u>.[9] And in this text, we are not talking about something, but about SOMEONE on whom we know we can rely. We know that we can trust Him because we can rely on **His character** just because of who He is. Some people say "He's the Lily of the Valley;" some say "He's the Bright and Morning Star;" some say "He's a Bridge over troubled water;" and I could go on and on with what some people say or have said…. but I want to remind us that first and foremost, He's Jesus, God's only begotten Son, born of the Virgin Mary, lived for 33 years, was denied by one disciple, betrayed by another; was illegally tried, found guilty, sentenced to die; was crucified, died and was buried, and was resurrected on the third day morning with all power in his hands, declaring that "I am He who lives, and was dead, and behold, I am alive forevermore."(*Revelation 1:18*). He's Jesus, the sacrificial lamb without spot or blemish; He's Jesus, the Savior of the world. That's His character.

Not only can we rely on His character, we know that we can trust Him because we can rely on **His ability**. We do have the assurance that He is able. The Bible says "…He is able to do exceedingly abundantly above all that we ask or think according to the power that works in us," *(Ephesians 3:20)*. Past practice and performance prove His ability to heal, set free and deliver. You already know the litany of His past performances…..He healed the sick; He made the blind to see; He made the deaf to hear; He made the lame to walk; He made the mute to talk; He fed the hungry; He cast out demons; He cleansed lepers; He caused fishing nets to be filled; He calmed raging seas; He walked on water, just to name some… Yes, we can trust Him implicitly. It makes no difference if there's nothing but darkness all around. Wait on Him and trust Him for "He is the Light of the World" (*John 8:12*) and "His word is a lamp to *our* feet and a light unto *our* path (*Psalm 119:105*) (*Italics mine*). It doesn't matter if we just can't seem to see our way clear, wait on Him and trust Him, and "walk *on* by faith and not by sight (*2 Corinthians 5:7*) (*Italics mine*)

Not only can we rely on His character and His ability, but we can trust Him because we can rely on **His strength.** In His strength "He gives power to the weak, and to those who have no might, He increases strength" (*Isaiah 40:29*); "He is the strength of *our* life" (*Psalm 27:1, Italics mine*); He is our refuge and strength, a very present help in trouble *(Psalm 46:1).*

We know that we can trust Him because we can rely on **His truth** and we can rely on His truth because He **is** truth *(John 14:6)* and His truth endures to all generations *(Psalm 100:5).*

Initially, I said that Trust is an assured reliance on the character, ability, strength, and truth of someone or something (and of course, in this text, we're talking about **someone)**. Just for your information, I'm a fan of acronyms, and taking notice of the first letters of the words **c**haracter, **a**bility, **s**trength, and **t**ruth—they form the word **CAST**. And that reminded me of *1 Peter 5:7* (**CAST**ing all your care upon Him for He cares for you).

It doesn't matter that we may not understand all the why's, the how's, and the wherefore's of how Jesus works, all we have to do is allow the Holy Spirit to bring to our remembrance Jesus' character, His ability, His strength, and His truth, and CAST all of our cares **upon** Him, take all of our burdens **to** Him; continue to wait **on** Him and trust **in** Him and then trust the process. The process produces miracles. Who can understand spitting on the ground, making clay of the spittle and rubbing it on blinded eyes then washing it off? The Bible says that after this process, the blind man came seeing." *(John 9:6,7)*

Who can understand how two small fish and five barley loaves would ever begin to feed a multitude of people The Bible says that this process of using that little boy's lunch fed 5,000 men plus women and children and still there were 12 baskets of fragments left over *(John 6:1-14).*

Who can really understand how someone who's been sick, unable to move for 38 years can suddenly, at the command of Jesus, get up and walk? *(John 5:5-9)* The Bible lets us know that this man who had been at the pool on his back on his bed now left the pool on his feet with his bed on his back—because he trusted the process, and the process produced a miracle.

Who can really understand the report of the text of this message---how water can be turned into wine without any human intervention? The Bible says that's exactly what happened, and that the new wine was better than the wine that had been served earlier (*John 2:10*). The process produced a miracle.

God still works miracles and if we fellowship with Him, if we have patience and wait on Him, and if we trust Him and obey Him, we'll see miracles manifested in our life. When it seems like the wine in your life runs out, when there seems to be no song in your soul, when there seems to be no hope in your heart, when there seems to be no smile on your lips, when there seems to be no joy in your spirit, fill up your water pots with whatever is ailing you and give them to Jesus, but give them to Him expecting a miracle. And He'll turn your water into wine.

BY ANY MEANS NECESSARY

⌘

Mark 2:1-12 (NKJV)

Mark 2:1-12

¹ And again He entered Capernaum after some days, and it was heard that He was in the house. ² Immediately many gathered together, so that there was no longer room to receive them, not even near the door. And He preached the word to them. ³ Then they came to Him, bringing a paralytic who was carried by four men. ⁴ And when they could not come near Him because of the crowd, they uncovered the roof where He was. So, when they had broken through, they let down the bed on which the paralytic was lying. ⁵ When Jesus saw their faith, He said to the paralytic, "Son, your sins are forgiven you." ⁶ And some of the scribes were sitting there and reasoning in their hearts, ⁷ "Why does this Man speak blasphemies like this? Who can forgive sins but God alone?" ⁸ But immediately, when Jesus perceived in His spirit that they reasoned thus within themselves, He said to them, "Why do you reason about these things in your hearts? ⁹ Which is easier, to say to the paralytic, 'Your sins are forgiven you,' or to say, 'Arise, take up your bed and walk'? ¹⁰ But that you may know that the Son of Man has power on earth to forgive sins"--He said to the paralytic, ¹¹ I say to you, arise, take up your bed, and go to your house." ¹² Immediately he arose, took up the bed, and went out in the presence of them all, so that all were amazed and glorified God, saying, "We never saw anything like this!"

"By any means necessary" is a translation of a phrase coined by the French intellectual Jean Paul Sartre in his play *Dirty Hands*. But I believe most of us are more familiar with its usage which came through a speech given by Malcolm X in 1965 which was the last year of his life. In that speech, in 1965, Malcom X said:

"We declare our right on this earth to be a man, to be a human being, to be respected as a human being, to be given the rights of a human being in this society, on this earth, in this day, which we intend to bring into existence by any means necessary." --Malcolm X, 1965

That phrase seemed to take on a life of its own and began to live and is still alive, for it is often heard in today's society in many different contexts. To say "by any means necessary" is generally considered to leave open all available tactics for the desired ends, including violence. However, the word "necessary" is the qualifier which adds a caveat—if violence is not necessary, then presumably, it should not be used.

In relating this subject to this text, it is not intended to promote violence as we know it—assaulting, shooting, stabbing, or in any way hurting anyone—but to advocate the use of strong, God-sanctioned tactics when approaching the throne of grace on behalf of others.

When we look at one portion of our society today (the portion of society in which seemingly unnecessary violence is being perpetrated continually), it would appear that the essence of that statement "by any means necessary" has been taken entirely too far. In some cases, what's being reported as minor arguments and disagreements is resulting in death caused by people who are seeking **resolution** to situations by any means necessary. In other situations, rejections by the object of one's affections are resulting in death caused by people who are seeking **revenge** by any means necessary. Payback for perceived mistreatment in employment situations is resulting in death (persons who are seeking **retaliation** by any means necessary). And unfortunately, a lot of this "stuff," this violence, isn't really a contemplated response to some perceived injustice or unfairness, but it's an in-the-moment knee-jerk reaction to somebody's unacceptable attitude or their unacceptable language, and unfortunately, "by any means necessary," lives are being snuffed out.

Then there is another portion of society who will not overstep the boundaries, and probably won't even go to the limits. These people have a laissez-faire or a live-and-let-live attitude: *"I don't care what you do so long as you don't bother me." "I don't care about what you need so long as you don't ask me for it." "I don't care where you go so long as you don't ask me to go with you."* While this attitude doesn't usually cause violent crimes to be committed against others, it does speak to one's unwillingness to stand up and be counted. It speaks to one's unwillingness to commit to a principle, or to go the extra mile, or to the Nth degree for a good cause. This seems to be true in any walk of their life.

In the marital relationship, men and women are more committed to self-gratification than they are committed to each other and the marriage. They seem to be in the relationship for what they can get, not for what they can give. They're looking out for #1 and when they don't get what they want, they walk out.

In the parental relationship, some mothers and fathers don't commit to the long-term and serious responsibilities that parenting demands. They're not willing to sacrifice the time and the energy it takes to lead and guide their children in the paths of righteousness. This is one of the reasons why so many of our young people are in trouble today. In many instances, some children, in too much of a hurry to grow up, are trying to act like adults, engaging in adult behaviors which in turn thrusts them into parenthood for which they are not ready. Ultimately, you have children trying to raise children. It doesn't work! Parents trying to be "pals" rather than parents. It doesn't work! Absentee fathers and resentful mothers inflicting verbal, emotional, and yes, physical abuse upon their children. It doesn't work! Parenting is a massive responsibility which (like the wedding vows) "is not to be entered into unadvisedly or lightly, but advisedly, seriously, soberly and in the fear of God." By any means necessary (within reason), mothers and fathers must take this responsibility seriously. God has entrusted parents with new life (lives)and the opportunity to shape and mold that life (lives) into productive and responsible human beings who will bring honor to God and to their family.

Then we look at the "friends" relationship. Many of those relationships leave a lot to be desired. There may be some who <u>can</u> claim "friends until the end," but more likely, you'll find the "fair-weather friends"—those who are with you as long as the weather is fair and sunny, and there are no problems, but who will make themselves scarce or even turn their back on you when the weather becomes cloudy and stormy and times become difficult. It's the "friends" relationship that we see demonstrated today in the text, not the "fair-weather friends," but the "through thick and thin friends" (as we used to say back in the day) the "all the way choo choo" friends.

In this message, some friends (in the King James version, Mark specifically says there were four), have a friend about whom they are sincerely concerned and who are willing to stick by this friend to the end….whatever it takes. By any means necessary. Matthew, Mark and Luke all tell this same story, but none of these Gospel writers give a lot of information about these men except to say that the one who needed healing was a paralytic, and that his four friends brought him to Jesus. They not only brought him to Jesus, but their plan was to make sure that he was noticed by Jesus. The Bible says that the house where Jesus was teaching was crowded and because of the crowd, they couldn't get their friend close enough to Jesus, so they had to try to <u>find</u> a way to get to Jesus. *(Mark 2:2-4)*

This situation reminded me of the story of Zacchaeus who wanted to see Jesus, who he was. He also couldn't get to see Jesus because he was short of stature and the crowd was a hindrance to him. But Zacchaeus didn't let his size, nor the crowd stop him. He was determined to see Jesus, so he ran on ahead of the crowd and climbed a sycamore tree where he was obviously able to get a better view of Jesus as He was passing by. That little exercise in creativity caused Zacchaeus to not only be noticed by Jesus, but to become Jesus' host for the day, for Jesus told Zacchaeus "come down… Today, I'm going to your house." *(Luke 19:1-10)*

Interesting also is the contrast between the story of this message and the story of the impotent man who was sick for 38 years. Apparently someone or some people had to have brought this impotent man to the pool, but by this man's own testimony, when he answered Jesus saying: "Sir, I have no one to put me into the pool when the water is stirred up…," *(John 5:7)* speaks to the fact that whoever brought him to the pool didn't stick around to help him when he really needed help *(John 5:1-9)*.

Not so in this message. These four friends had a purpose—to get their friend to Jesus and to stay with him. They planned as to how to get him to Jesus. There is indeed something to be said for having a purpose and a positive plan for if one is determined, then, by any means necessary, they will not let anything or anyone stop them from doing what they have to do. Zacchaeus was not prevented from seeing Jesus by his physical challenge of being short, nor was he prevented by the crowd. Neither were these four men. These men (these friends, if you will) had a purpose and their purpose was to get their friend to Jesus, and they did not allow the crowd to prevent them from carrying out their plan and achieving their purpose.

Although this crowd seemed rather foreboding, there <u>are</u> times when a crowd does have its place. A crowd is a group of people who may have a common purpose and have come together for a specific cause, such as a political rally, a sports game, or a church service. Or it might be a gathering of folk who are ready to protest and show solidarity against an establishment or an issue with which they're in disagreement. Sometimes, some people feel safe in a crowd while others may feel overwhelmed by a crowd. Sometimes crowds tend to become noisy, and while some people are happy to join in the noisemaking and rabble-rousing, others would rather stay off to themselves in a quieter atmosphere. Unfortunately, however, whether it's a large crowd, a small crowd, a quiet crowd, a loud crowd, a protesting crowd, a shouting crowd or even just a listening crowd, crowds can be intimidating, especially when it seems like the crowd is prohibitive and represents a barrier that stands between them and someone or something else. It's at these times when some of us allow the crowd to deter us or prevent us from doing what we have planned to do. When we look up and see the crowd, our own mission sometimes becomes misty, our purpose gets polluted, our plan gets pushed aside and we begin to have second thoughts. Doubts begin to creep in; we hang back or we turn back completely and allow ourselves to be intimidated and deterred from what we were going to do.

This was not so with these four friends. When they arrived at the house where Jesus was teaching, and realized that they couldn't get through the crowd of people to Jesus, they might have said (using today's vernacular), *"OK, my brothers, we can't get him to Jesus through this crowd, but we know there's more than one way to skin a cat, don't we?"* We also need to understand that there is more than one way to get to Jesus. The Bible says that there's only one way to God, and that's through Jesus. Jesus, himself, backs that up by saying "I am the way, the truth and the life; no one comes to the Father except through Me." (*John 14:6*). On the other hand, however, there is more than one way to come to Jesus. Now someone might want to raise the question here: "What is the difference? Aren't we taught that God, the Father, God, the Son, and God the Holy Spirit are the Trinity—the Three in One? How can there be a distinction made between how one comes to God and how one comes to Jesus? In answer to this question, yes, indeed, this is the teaching: God, the Father, God, the Son, and God the Holy Spirit are "Three in One", but understand that they are "three persons, three entities with three separate functions all in the One God. God, the Father is the one who created us and is the source of everything. In the beginning when Adam and Eve sinned and fell from grace, God had a plan to redeem and reconcile humankind back to Him. Thus, God sent His Son, Jesus, as the implementer of that plan and God, the Son is the one who calls us to come to Him and He's the one who redeems, saves from sin, and reconciles humankind with God, the Father. God, the Holy Spirit is the one whom the Son sent to be a comforter and a sustainer after He went back to His Father. God the Holy Spirit is the one who convicts people and causes them to answer the call of Jesus, then He also comforts and sustains them. So, yes, a distinction is made in how one comes to the Father. One comes to the Father only through the Son (Jesus) by the power of the Holy Spirit. However, everybody doesn't answer the call to come to Jesus in just one way. Everybody doesn't come to Jesus walking down the aisle of a church on Sunday morning. Through the media of Televangelism, some have come, and still may come to Jesus at home on a Tuesday night. Through Street Evangelistic Ministries, some have come, and still may come to Jesus on the street on a Saturday afternoon. Through Ministerial Visitation Ministries, some have come, and still may come to Jesus on their hospital, hospice, and/or convalescent home beds on any given day. Through Prison Ministries, some have come, and still may come to Jesus while incarcerated in their jail cells. It is indeed a blessing that such outreach ministries exist and are ready, willing and able to reach out to the least, the lost, and the left out, and **by any means necessary**, try to bring them in to Jesus. One of the old hymns of the church has these words: *"Bring them in, bring them in, Bring them in from the fields of sin; Bring them in, bring them in, Bring the wand'ring ones to Jesus."*[10]

The four friends sought to bring their friend to Jesus **by any means necessary**. It isn't clear just what may have given them the idea to go up and let him down through the roof. It could have been that using this means of access was common in those days. You see, it wouldn't have been a situation then like the image that has probably come to your mind now. Today we think of a house with a roof that is made up of asphalt shingles firmly secured to the top of the house with roofing nails. And most houses today don't have outside steps leading up to the roof. This is not a reference to those building that have fire escapes, but rather private homes. So, to our way of thinking, to try to remove part of that roof would probably be time-consuming and problematic. However, we really can't think about this situation in terms of today's culture. It was a much different situation back then. In that culture, in Palestine, the roof of a house was flat and was regularly used as a place of rest and quiet. There was usually an outside stairway which led up to the roof. The roof consisted of flat beams laid across from wall to wall about three feet apart. That three-foot space was filled with brushwood packed tight with clay. Then it was covered over with *Marl* which is a fine-grained sedimentary rock consisting of clay minerals. Then, on top of this mixture of soil and clay, grass grew, and to unroof the roof (so to speak) was not a difficult task to perform. Just a matter of digging out the filling between two of the beams.[11] This is precisely what these men did, and after ensuring that the space they dug out was wide enough, they presented their friend down through the space directly in front of Jesus.

The Bible doesn't specifically address this, but if you use your imagination just a little bit, can't you see the looks of surprise and maybe shock on the faces of some of those in the crowd down below when they looked up and saw this man being lowered to ground? More than likely, this was an unusual and unexpected turn of events, and no doubt, some of the folk became perplexed and puzzled by this action and may have had some negative reactions. Their reactions may have been a little like the reactions that some folk have today when they see the people of God do unusual and unexpected things. People are often puzzled when they see genuine, honest-to-goodness believers who love their enemies, who do not react to, but rather respond with blessings for those who curse them. They're puzzled when they see people who do not retaliate negatively but rather do good to them who hate them, and who pray for those who spitefully use them and persecute them. They can't seem to understand a believer who, during chaotic situations demonstrate the peace of God that surpasses all understanding. They get confused and rattled when situation after situation has a negative impact and sometimes devastating results, and still the believer testifies, believes, and stands firm on the Word that says "all things work together for good to those who love God, to those who are the called according to His purpose" *(Romans 8:28)*. Even in many churches, there are sometimes puzzled and perplexed looks of surprise when, under the anointing of the Holy Spirit, the pastor prays for and lays hands on folk and they fall under that anointing. Yes, some of those in the crowd might have been puzzled to see these four men presenting their friend down through the roof to get him to Jesus. Yet, this kind of perseverance on the part of this sick man's friends was proof of their faith. The Bible says, **"when Jesus saw their faith,** He said to the paralytic, "son, your sins are forgiven you." *(Mark 2:5)*

Now, we shall digress momentarily, and take a little side trip to take a deeper look at the words of this phrase: **"when Jesus saw their faith?"** First, the emphasis will be on the fact that Jesus **SAW** their faith. Ordinarily, it's thought that one can't actually see faith because faith is an intangible; it's invisible and not seen with the physical eye. However, one can see the results of faith. It's kind of like the wind. We can't see the wind, but we see the results of what the wind does. When the wind blows, leaves and limbs of trees move. Paper and other light debris are scattered all around. We can see that and therefore we know that the wind is in operation. Inanimate objects that are not secured will move and even get caught up in the wind. We can see that. As human individuals, we can also feel the wind on our faces, and when the wind blows with high intensity, we, ourselves, are sometimes carried along by the force with which the wind is blowing. We can feel all of that, but through it all, we really can't see the wind, itself. So, it is with faith. We can't really see one's faith, but we can see the actions and demonstrations that actually make one's faith visible and tangible to those around us.

When a high school senior appears to not have the necessary funds to go to college, but in spite of that, he or she goes right ahead and applies to the colleges, applies for the scholarships and the financial aid, and completes and submits (on time) all the necessary paperwork in the face of this seeming impossibility, that's when we see his or her faith.

When one goes to apply for a job and it seems like every door is closed and every avenue they thought was opened to them turned out to be a dead end, and yet, they hear of still another opportunity, they get up, get dressed, wipe away the tears, put on a happy face, and go out and try again. That's when others see their faith.

When it's coming down toward the end of the month but there's still more month left than money, and a mother isn't quite sure how she's going to feed her children their supper, but she goes ahead and puts a pot of water on the stove, sets the table anyhow, and sits down and asks God's blessings on what they're about to receive—that's when others see her faith.

Even in the church, when plans and programs are being hindered by those who are standing on the side lines saying "no, you can't," but still the pastor takes the two or three who stand with him or her and say "yes, we can," and they press toward the goal for the prize of the upward call of God in Christ Jesus *(Philippians 3:14)*, that's when others see their faith, and not just others, but most importantly, God sees that faith. He sees those actions; He sees the moves that are made; He sees the steps that are taken and He knows that they're not walking by sight, but walking by faith *(2 Corinthians 5:7- paraphrased)* and He honors that faith walk.

So, it was with these four friends. They couldn't get through the crowd, so they took their sick friend up on the roof, made a hole in the roof, and let him down at the feet of Jesus, and Jesus saw their faith.

Then the phrase says Jesus saw **THEIR** faith. Not the faith of the man who was paralyzed, but **THEIR** faith—the faith of his friends. Not the faith of the one who needed to be healed, but the faith of those who wanted him to be healed. Not the faith of the one who was brought to Jesus, but the faith of the ones who brought him to Jesus. This should be a great source of encouragement to caregivers, intercessors, prayer warriors, and all of those who stand in the gap for others. Although it seems that Jesus gave an immediate response to this situation in this text, sometimes our answers don't come so quickly, and we may begin to wonder if our efforts on behalf of others will bring about the desired results. We may wonder if our prayers for others are effective; we may wonder if our faith is enough to reach the saving, healing, merciful, delivering heart of God. We may even wonder if the person for whom we're praying shouldn't demonstrate their faith as well. After all, we are familiar with the story of the blind men who wanted to see, and Jesus said: "according to **YOUR FAITH**, it will be done for you." *(Matthew 9:28)* We're also familiar with the story of the woman with the issue of blood who was healed and Jesus telling her that **HER FAITH** had made her well (*Luke 8:40-50 - paraphrased*). Yet, juxtaposed with that same story, we see that a 12-year-old girl was raised from the dead (*Luke 8:41, 42*), and, of course, it wasn't her faith (because she was dead); no, it wasn't her faith, but Jesus had told her father, "…only believe, and she will be made well." (*Luke 8:50*) There's really no set formula. It's according to the situation, and most of all it's according to the will of almighty God. If you're praying for an unsaved loved one, that person cannot demonstrate a faith that he or she does not have. If you're praying for the sick, they may be so sick (perhaps in a coma), that they cannot demonstrate their faith at that time. If you're praying for someone who is bound by some of the "chains" of this life, that person may be so confused and befuddled that they can't walk in faith for their deliverance. So, God has caregivers, intercessors, and prayer warriors in place to stand in the gap for them. And if you're one whom God has put in position to intercede on behalf of others, then you must be ready to go the extra mile. You must be ready to demonstrate **your** faith through **persistence and perseverance**. The Bible says "without faith it is impossible to please Him, for he who comes to God must believe that He is, and that He is a rewarder of those who diligently seek Him" (*Hebrews 11:6*). Be advised that "diligent" is the operative word here. The dictionary says that **Diligent means to *be "constant in an effort to accomplish something; to be attentive and persistent in doing something***."[12] Biblically, that sounds remarkably familiar. *1 Thessalonians 5:17, 18,* tells us to "pray without ceasing." *Ephesians 6:17* says: "praying always with all prayer and supplication in the Spirit, being watchful to this end with all perseverance and supplication for all the saints." Paul tells Timothy (*2 Timothy 4:2*) to "Preach the word! Be ready in season and out of season. Convince, rebuke, exhort with all longsuffering." Whatever way we want to say it, being persistent, persevering, diligently seeking God on behalf of others—this is a demonstration of our faith and in due season will bring a response from our Father. However, in our persistence, in our perseverance, sometimes we must be ready, willing, and able to come out of the box, so to speak, to come out of our comfort zone and go the extra mile. We may have to get out of the boat and walk on the water a little bit. We may have to turn our plate down, lay prostrate before the Lord and fast and pray for a while (*Matthew 17:21*). We may have to do some wrestling with God all night long, and tell Him, as Jacob did, that we won't let Him go until He blesses us (*Genesis 32:26 - paraphrased*). We may have to climb a tree and go out on a limb for a minute (*Luke 19:4 - paraphrased*). We may have to do whatever we have to do...... **by any means necessary**.

Sometimes some of us want to be cute when it's time to pray. We want to be proper, use the proper words, use the proper form, get in the proper posture, and position, and use the proper protocol. Some folk want to display their eloquence and their skills of elocution. And...there's nothing wrong with using proper form and protocol; there's nothing wrong in showing what you know, but there is a time and a place to show what you know.

In the college/university/seminary classroom, it's ok. As a matter of fact, it's good for us to try to impress our professor with what we've learned. We can go ahead and let him or her know that in the construction of our sermons, we utilized a wonderful homiletical device known as the Hegelian dialectic of thesis, antithesis, and synthesis. And if our utilization of that device was efficacious, it might put an "A" on our report card and help us toward a 4.0 GPA.

In the executive board room, it's good to try to wow our colleagues with our verbosity and intelligence. That might get us a raise and a corner office.

In the convention room, we can use the established protocol—give honor to God and acknowledge everybody from the president to the parking lot attendant if we want to; but...in the prayer room, we really have to get real and be real. God's not impressed by our intelligence; He's not edified by our eloquence; He's not persuaded by our use of proper protocol. We may have to cry a little; our nose may cause us to sniffle; we may use some Ebonics instead of the King's English; we may split some infinitives and dangle some participles; but if our prayer cry is from the heart, this is what touches the heart of God. He is touched by a humbled spirit and a contrite heart (*Psalm 51:17- paraphrased*). He's touched by our realness; He's touched by our sincerity; He's touched by our humility. He's touched by the diligence with which we seek Him. He says, "if My people who are called by My name will humble themselves and pray and seek My face, and turn from their wicked ways, then I will hear from heaven, I will forgive their sin, and heal their land." (*2 Chronicles 7:14*). Sometimes we must lay aside those weights of primness, properness, and protocol, come out of the box, and just keep it real!

Finally, He's touched by our faith. The text says Jesus saw their **FAITH**. Remember the progression: He **SAW**, their faith; He saw **THEIR** faith. The emphasis is now on **FAITH**. When He saw their faith, He said to the paralytic, "son, your sins are forgiven you." *(Mark 2:5)* The Bible says: "Now faith is the substance of things hoped for, the evidence of things not seen" *(Hebrews 11:1)*. Jesus saw them showing the substance of what they were hoping for; He saw them exhibiting the evidence of what they had not yet seen. He saw them acting on what they believed would happen although it had not yet happened. They obviously believed that if they could just get their friend to Jesus, that he would be healed, and they were willing to uphold their belief **by any means necessary.**

Not only was the result achieved (physical healing), but in the interim, Jesus forgave the man with the paralysis of his sins. While this man did not confess any sins, Jesus, in His infinite wisdom, knew that this man was not only paralyzed physically, but he was paralyzed spiritually. He couldn't walk and he didn't know Jesus, and in His infinite mercy, Jesus was more concerned about his spiritual health than his physical health. In other words, this text is letting us know that a healthy spiritual condition will lead to a healthy physical condition.

In our own lives, sometimes physical healing is hindered due to sin in our lives, and we, who know Jesus as Lord and Savior, are admonished to confess any known sin that we might be forgiven and cleansed of all unrighteousness *(1 John 1:9-paraphrased)*. Be advised that we can't fool God. He knows our heart; He knows our mind; He knows our conditions; He knows what we need and when we need it. Thus, we would do well to be obedient to His word—"confess our trespasses to one another, and pray for one another, that you may be healed." *(James 5:16)*. This is not a formula for healing. Students of the Bible know that healing comes to different people in different ways on a case by case basis; nevertheless, better to read and obey God's word and put yourself in position to expect a miracle, rather than function in ignorance and disobedience and find yourself asking the question over and over again: "Why can't I get healed?"

After forgiving the man of his sins, Jesus told the man to "...arise, take up your bed and go to your house." *(Mark 2:11)* The man got up and went home, indicating that his healing was complete. He was spiritually healed and physically healed.

The four friends' plan, purpose, and mission for their friend was accomplished by the means they felt necessary, and we, as believers in the Lord Jesus Christ, have the same responsibility as these four friends. Are you aware of a situation or some situations that are going to require more than a "now I lay me down to sleep; I pray the Lord my soul to keep" prayer? Is there someone in your life who's going through something and for them, you might have to go that extra mile to help bring them through that something? Is there someone you know who needs a touch from the Master, and the responsibility is falling on you to provide the means necessary to get them to Jesus to get that touch? Is there somebody for whom you have to un-roof the roof?

If your answer to these questions is "Yes", and you think you might have some difficulty in going to bat for them; you think you might have some difficulty in going the extra mile to resolve the situation; you think you might have some difficulty in coming out of your comfort zone, then your best course of action is to look to Jesus who is the author and finisher of our faith (*Hebrews 12:2- paraphrased*). Look to Jesus, the One who thought it not robbery to use whatever means necessary to reconcile fallen humankind back to His Father. The means necessary for our reconciliation **with the Father** was His momentary alienation **from the Father**—hear Him saying "My God, My God, why have You forsaken me?" (*Matthew 27:46*). The means necessary for our cleansing from sin and ultimate salvation was His suffering and shame and the shedding of His precious blood. The means necessary for our becoming a new creation was His crucifixion on an old rugged cross. The means necessary for our healing were the wounds that He endured for our transgressions and the bruises that He endured for our iniquities. The means necessary for securing our peace was the chastisement that was put upon Him, and with the stripes that caused those wounds and bruises, we are healed (*Isaiah 53:5 -paraphrased*), and not only have we been reconciled, but we now have **peace with God**, and the **peace of God** that surpasses all understanding.

Nevertheless, I don't want to leave Jesus there on the cross in a wounded and bruised condition, because that's not the end of the story. Yes He was crucified, Yes He died and was buried, but, the means necessary for us to live an abundant life here and now, and to have eternal life in the hereafter was for God to raise Jesus from the dead which He did on the third day morning, and now, because He lives, we too shall live; because He lives, we must use whatever means necessary to bring somebody to meet the living Lord. Because He lives, we can use whatever means necessary to introduce somebody to the resurrected savior. *"Because He lives, we can face tomorrow (and all that tomorrow entails). Because He lives, all fear is gone; because we know Who holds tomorrow, and life is worth the living, just because He lives."*[13]

CAN YOU C.O.P.E. WITH YOUR JERICHO?"

～∞∞∞～

Joshua 6:1-5 (NKJV)

¹ Now Jericho was securely shut up because of the children of Israel; none went out, and none came in. ² And the LORD said to Joshua: "See! I have given Jericho into your hand, its king, and the mighty men of valor. ³ You shall march around the city, all you men of war; you shall go all around the city once. This you shall do six days. ⁴ And seven priests shall bear seven trumpets of rams' horns before the ark. But the seventh day you shall march around the city seven times, and the priests shall blow the trumpets. ⁵ It shall come to pass, when they make a long blast with the ram's horn, and when you hear the sound of the trumpet, that all the people shall shout with a great shout; then the wall of the city will fall down flat. And the people shall go up every man straight before him."

A brief background of this story reveals that the Israelites had already come a long way. They had been miraculously delivered from their bondage in Egypt; they had wandered in the wilderness for 40 years, and in all their wilderness wanderings, God had continually supplied their needs. They had miraculously crossed over the Jordan on their way to the Promised Land. God had told them to go in and conquer all the cities of Canaan and possess the land, and the primary obstacle was this fortified city called Jericho—one of the oldest cities in the world, and in some places, had fortified walls that were up to 25 feet high and 20 feet thick. Jericho was a symbol of military power and strength, but a symbol was really all it was for "the Lord said to Joshua, 'See, I have given Jericho into your hand, its king, and the mighty men of valor." *(Joshua 6:2)* God told Joshua that Jericho, with its King and all its mighty men of valor were already defeated. These must have been encouraging words to Joshua—to know that the victory was already theirs. God had said it; all he had to do was believe it, accept it, and act on it. We would be more victorious in our own lives if we would believe God's Word, accept God's Word, and act on God's Word.

God gave Joshua his instructions for battle, telling him that the entire army was to walk around the city once a day for six days. Behind the army, seven priests were to walk ahead of the Ark of the Covenant, each priest carrying a trumpet made from a ram's horn. On the seventh day, they were to walk around the city seven times, and the priests were to blow their trumpets. Then, when the priests gave one long loud blast on the trumpets, all the people were to give a mighty shout and the walls of the city would fall flat.

Someone might be asking the question: "If they already had the victory, if the enemy had already been defeated, then why did God give Joshua all these elaborate and precise instructions for battle? I suggest that you might want to consider those situations in your own life where you already know the result, but you've still got to take the necessary steps to obtain that result. For instance, you probably know what you're going to have for supper tonight; you may already know that you're going to be victorious over that hunger that will attack around 4 or 5 o'clock this afternoon, but you've still got to make some preparations. You still must prepare your meat, potatoes, and vegetables, cook them, and then set your table with the necessary eating utensils, then serve the meal before you can see the result in readiness for eating. *(Note: On a Sunday, many of us may not go through all that preparation process, but rather go out to the restaurant and wait to be served. Nevertheless, whether it's elaborate preparation or just a quick trip to the restaurant, you know that you will be victorious over that hunger).* So, it was with Joshua. He knew that the victory was his, but he had to prepare, and Joshua wasn't really preparing for battle, but for victory. God had already given him the city; he just had to prepare to go in and take it.

This is some of our problem today. We prepare for battle with fear and trembling when we should prepare for victory through faith and trust. It's an "already, but not yet" process, a process similar to the salvation experience. Believers already have the victory, but the battle is not yet over. Believers have already been saved by the blood of the Lamb; the devil has already been defeated, but they've not yet reached the promised land. We must continue to keep on the whole armor; we must continue to hold up the blood-stained banner; we must continue to walk on and fight by faith; nevertheless, we **have** the victory by our belief in the Captain of our salvation.

In this life, we are going to come upon our own individual "Jericho"— not a literal fortified city, but some problem or difficulty that appears to be an extremely large obstacle, and we'll feel like we can't cope with it. If we live long enough, we will run into mountains that seem to be unclimbable; we'll come upon rivers that seem to be uncrossable; we'll enter wildernesses that seem to be impenetrable, but if we have truly been saved by the blood of the lamb, then we must have **CONFIDENCE** in the God of our salvation. (This is the C in the main word of this message: COPE). We must be confident that this problem, whatever it is, is just one of those "already but not yet" problems; be confident that we've already got the answer, but we still have to go through the process to realize it—we still have to go through the trauma of the problem before we can experience the transition to victory. We must still go through the process in preparation for the victory. We demonstrate this confidence by being still and seeing the salvation of the Lord; by being still and hearing words of encouragement to our heart… "your enemy has already been defeated; I've already given you the victory." If your "Jericho" is sickness, be still and hear Him speak through the words of scripture: "by His stripes you are healed" (*Isaiah 53).* If your "Jericho" is unemployment, be still and hear the words of scripture: "And my God shall supply all your need according to His riches in glory by Christ Jesus." (*Philippians 4:19).* If your "Jericho" is depression (for one reason or another), be still and hear Jesus say: "Come unto me all you who labor and are heavy-laden, and I will give you rest" (*Matthew 11:28).* If your "Jericho" is loneliness and lonesomeness because it seems that everyone has turned their back on you, be still and take comfort in the promise: "Lo, I am with you always…" *(Matthew 28:19).* "I will never leave you nor forsake you" (*Hebrews 13:5).* We are children of the King, and as Kings Kids, we can be confident that our Father has already given us the victory over our "Jerichos."

Joshua had this confidence and he continued to listen to the instructions from the Lord. The instructions that God gave Joshua, from a human perspective, seemed strange and unusual, and actually seemed to be inadequate for such an undertaking. They were to walk around the wall, and the wall would fall. Ordinarily, to achieve such an undertaking, one would expect to be instructed to have the men dig trenches to try to tunnel under the wall, or to get ladders and climb over the wall, or to have them draw up battering rams to knock down the wall, or at the very least, to formulate some secret military strategy. But this was not so with Joshua. His instructions were to walk around the city for seven days. These instructions, according to our finite way of thinking, definitely do not make sense. However, we must realize that "our ways are not God's ways " (*Isaiah 55: 8b - paraphrased*) and what we *think* about the instructions isn't really important; it's how we *respond* to the instructions, and Joshua responded in **OBEDIENCE**. (This is the O in COPE).

Joshua probably could have done what some of us would do if faced with this same situation. He could have called a meeting with his executive council—the heads of all the tribes—and asked for their advice and suggestions. But of course, with twelve tribes, there would have been twelve different opinions...everybody "leaning unto their own understanding." (*Proverbs 3: 5b - paraphrased*). But even in the face of this hard-to-understand command, Captain Joshua knew that these were God-given instructions and he didn't defer to human suggestion but chose to be obedient to Divine direction.

We must also learn to be obedient if we are to realize the victory that we've already won. Too often we go to others to ask for their advice, their opinions, and their suggestions, but in the long run, listening to a lot of outside advice only causes more confusion. We need to take our burdens to the Lord, ask the Savior to help us, confident that He is willing to help us, and that He will bring us through whatever we're going through. And when He does come to our aid, when He does give us instructions for the task, whether we fully understand them or not, our best recourse is to listen, trust, and obey. Like Joshua, we must realize that God-given instructions are to be obeyed and not questioned. As I said before, God's ways are not our ways, and His thoughts are not our thoughts (*Isaiah 55: 8 - paraphrased*), and the limitations of our humanity prevent us from seeing and understanding the wide scope of His Divinity. God has always, and still, moves in mysterious ways, His wonders to perform. We cannot and will not understand everything that God says or does. Although we have read the account in Biblical history, can we really understand how this world came into being from the mouth of God? Can we really understand how God stepped out on space, reached back into nowhere, grabbed a handful of nothing, and made a whole lot of something—heaven and earth; sea and sky; sun, moon, and stars; light and darkness, fields and streams, trees and grass, animals, fish and fowl—can we really understand this? Can we understand how a black angus cow can eat green grass and give white milk? Do we really understand how the microscopic seed of a man unites with the egg of a woman, and in nine months, a fully-developed human being weighing anywhere from 5 – 9 pounds (sometimes less and sometimes more), is brought into the world having physical and mental characteristics as well as personalities of both his or her mother and father? Can we really understand how—when a vegetable or flower seed is planted in the ground, and when watered and given sunlight, in about six weeks, the beginning of food or flowers comes forth? No! Despite all the scientific research, we don't completely understand these phenomena, and what's more, we don't question it; we accept all of it as a matter of course, as a part of life. So then, why question a difficult to understand instruction from the Lord that will ultimately help us to conquer our "Jericho?" Why not just believe, trust, and obey?

As we consider the text of this message again, we see that as the army of the Israelites was to march around the city, they were to take with them the Ark of the Covenant. The Ark was Israel's most prized possession. It was a symbol of God's presence and His power. Physically, the Ark was a rectangular box. On the lid of the box were two cherubim facing each other. Inside the box were the tablets on which the Ten Commandments were written which Moses had received from God, a jar of Manna—the bread that God had sent down from heaven when they were in the wilderness; and Aaron's staff which was a symbol of the High Priests' authority. To carry the Ark of the Covenant in their midst was to be assured of God's presence and His power to deliver. This should be a source of encouragement to us. Sometimes, when we encounter difficulty, we may not always have a visible sign or symbol of God's presence, but as believers, if we have been obedient and hidden the Word in our heart, the Holy Spirit will bring to our remembrance the very symbols of His presence and power that we need. As a reminder, the Psalmist said: "God is our refuge and strength, a very present help in trouble" *(Psalm 46:1)*. He said that "The Lord is my light and my salvation, whom shall I fear? The Lord is the strength of my life, of whom shall I be afraid. When the wicked came against me To eat up my flesh, My enemies and foes, They stumbled and fell." *(Psalm 27:1,2)* Isaiah gives the encouraging reminder that says: "When you pass through the waters, I will be with you, And through the waters, they shall not overflow you. When you walk through the fire, you shall not be burned, Nor shall the flame scorch you." *(Isaiah 43:2)*. And David, from his own experience says: "Yea, though I walk through the valley of the shadow of death, I will fear no evil; For You are with me; Your rod and Your staff, they comfort me." *(Psalm 23:4)*.

God's Word in our heart is our symbol of God's presence with us, and "…the word of God is living and powerful and sharper than any two-edged sword" *(Hebrews 4:12)*, and that same word says: "…He who is in you is greater than he who is in the world." *(1 John 4:4)*, and "if God is for us, who can be against us?" *(Romans 8:31)*.

Joshua's orders were to march around the city once every day for six days and seven times on the seventh day. Overall, from our human perspective, there just does not seem to be any rhyme or reason to these instructions. After all, they were on the verge of battle and whoever heard of a mighty fortress being captured by talking a walk? Previously, they were told to conquer the city and possess the land; now their orders are simply to walk around the city for seven days. I imagine the inhabitants in the city were probably watching them, waiting for them to make an authentic military maneuver, and can you imagine their surprise and probable confusion when all Joshua and his people did was walk around the city every day at the same time. The Israelites themselves were not even told what the result would be. They were just instructed to walk around the city for seven days.

This really must have been an exercise in **PATIENCE and PERSISTENCE** (This is the P in COPE)—They had to have <u>patience</u> to carry out the instructions (whether they understood them or not), and the <u>persistence</u> to keep on doing what they had been told to do. From this scenario, we might learn a lesson. We learn that not only are God's ways not our ways, but God's time is not our time. He moves in His time and we would do well to fit our time into His time. When we are facing our "Jericho," and the walls are not coming down when we want them to, we must learn to be patient. He may not come when we want Him, but when He comes, He's comes in time and on time. When we remember the story of Lazarus, although Jesus seemed to be too late getting to the grave, He was still on time. Too often, when things don't happen when we want them to, or the way we want them to, we are prone to become disappointed and frustrated, and we step back and/or give up. Sometimes, however, God's timing is a test of our patience, persistence and our perseverance, probably intended to find out just how much **confidence** we really do have in Him, and if we're willing to continue to be **obedient** no matter what happens.

Picture now and use your sanctified imagination with me as we look at the Israelites as they're preparing to walk around the city. I don't know what day it was when they started out, but I imagine that day #1 probably wasn't so bad. When we start a new project, even one that we're not fond of, it isn't so bad at the beginning. As a matter of fact, it might even be a little exciting because it's something new. So, they walked around as they had been instructed and went on back to camp. Then came day #2, and they got up early and again walked around the city according to their instructions, and then went on back to camp. Then day #3, I imagine that now some of the newness was getting old; the enthusiasm was wearing off, and the Israelites were probably becoming a bit disgruntled. You know the history of the Israelites back when Moses was their leader. They constantly moaned and groaned and complained. Every time things didn't go their way, they would turn against Moses. And although the older generations had died out, *you know the old saying: the apple doesn't fall far from the tree,* and I imagine this generation probably did their share of complaining also. However, if they did, it had to be done on the down low, after they completed their trip around the city, for Joshua had instructed them to be completely silent as they walked (except for blowing of the trumpets).

How often do we, in our ministries, complain about this and criticize that, knocking this program and talking negatively about that ministry? It would behoove us to be quiet for a while and go ahead and discharge our duties in silence. People have often missed their blessings because they've been talking instead of listening and/or working. Not only must we be still, but sometimes, we must also be silent so that we can see the salvation of the Lord.

Now day #4 has arrived. The Bible doesn't say this, but in my sanctified imagination, I wonder if, after they returned to camp on this day, a few members of each tribe may have gotten together and began to discuss the situation. You know how we do sometimes. They probably asked each other: "Just what does Joshua think he's doing anyhow? What does he think is supposed to be accomplished by getting up every morning and walking around the city? When are we going to stop all this nonsense and get on with the battle to conquer the city?" Somebody else might even have said, "Now, if I were captain of this army, I know how I'd handle this thing. I know what strategy I'd use." Somebody in the organization or in the ministry always thinks they have a better idea than the president. Somebody in the church thinks they have a better plan or program than the Pastor. Somebody always thinks they have a better way of doing something. And so, I just imagine that in typical Israelite fashion, they began to complain.

Now we come to day #5, and after their trip around the city and their return to camp on that day, (and I'm still using my imagination), I think another group of tribesman may have come together and began to make plans to get rid of Joshua. "Joshua doesn't know what he's doing; all this walking around isn't doing anything, and we need to get somebody in who knows how to be a leader—somebody who really knows how to get this party started and get things moving."

And now on day #6, although it was next to the last day, I think another group might have gotten together to make plans for a strike. I hear the leader of this group saying: "I'm not walking around this city anymore. I've walked around this city for six days. The next walk I take, I'm walking out! Is anybody walking with me?" But then I hear somebody else saying, "Now wait just a minute, brothers. We've already walked around the city for these six days and tomorrow is the last day. Why don't we just go on and see what the end will be? No, I don't know for sure what's going to happen tomorrow, and I don't know where we're going, but I certainly know where we've been and how far we've come. We've been through a lot, my brothers, and we've come too far to stop now. Why don't we just hold on and see what tomorrow will bring?"

It's often this way in our own lives. Sometimes when we don't get the answers to our questions, when we can't see the solutions to our problems, we tend to give up and back off from our goals. But in times like these, we might do well to remember the words of the hymn writer who said: "*Trials dark on every hand, and we cannot understand all the ways that God would lead us to that blessed promised land; but He guides us with His eye, and we'll follow 'til we die, and we'll understand it better bye and by.*"[14] Yes, I imagine that there was a voice of reason, a voice of encouragement that might have come forth to give the others a little push to press on.

Well, day #7 arrived and on this day, according to the instructions, instead of marching around the city once, they were to march around seven times and the seventh time, give a great shout. Now, In God's mathematics, the #7 means completion, divine perfection, and students of the Bible, are familiar with the myriad of references to the #7. 7 days in a week; 7 notes in the musical scale; Jacob worked 7 years for his wife; his father-in-law tricked him, and he had to work 7 more years to get the wife he wanted in the first place; when the Hebrew boys were put into the furnace, the furnace had been heated 7 times hotter than usual; Naaman the leper was told to go wash 7 times in Jordan and he would be cleansed of his leprosy; Jesus spoke 7 last words from the cross. In the Book of Revelation, 7 angels, 7 churches, 7 dooms, 7 golden candlesticks, 7 lamps of fire, 7 seals, 7 spirits of God, 7 stars, 7 thunders, 7 trumpets. The #7 has great significance and in obedience to their instructions, the Israelis Army marched around the city seven times on the seventh day, and as they marched, again in my sanctified imagination, I think they began to remember the victories they had already won.

*As they marched around one time, they may have remembered Moses who had been their first leader. *As they marched around the second time, they may have remembered their deliverance from Pharaoh and their bondage in Egypt. *As they marched around the third time, they may have remembered their miraculous passage through the Red Sea on dry land. *As they marched around the fourth time, maybe they remembered the pillar of cloud by day, and the pillar of fire by night which led them while in the wilderness. *As they marched around the fifth time, they may have remembered their continual blessings while in the wilderness—for forty years they had clothes on their backs, their shoes never wore out, and they were never hungry. *As they marched around the sixth time, maybe they remembered crossing over Jordan. *And now they're marching around the seventh time in preparation to go in and possess the land.

The Bible says that when the people heard the trumpet blast, they shouted as loud as they could—in other words, you might say, they got **EXCITED** (this is the E in COPE), and suddenly, the walls of Jericho crumbled and fell before them, and the people of Israel poured in from every side and captured the city.

Notice, if you will, the order of events. They didn't wait for the walls to fall before they shouted. They didn't wait until it was all over before they shouted; They didn't wait to see the victory before they shouted. According to their instructions, they shouted first, and then the walls fell. We're not told what they shouted, and as I thought about this, I have wondered if the SHOUT, in and of itself, might have been the non-verbal command for the walls to fall!!! You know when we shout, many times we might say different things…. somebody may shout- HALLELUJAH! Somebody else may shout GLORY! Somebody else may shout – THANK YOU JESUS! And so, it can be in our own lives, and I suggest that now you make this personal. When you find yourself confronted by a "Jericho Wall," believe that you can figuratively do as the Israelites did—walk around that wall one day at a time, and no matter how much, or how large an obstacle that wall seems to be, stand strong in the conviction that "with God all things are possible" (Matthew 19:26) and that with Him, you can C.O.P.E. with this situation, whatever it is. You can be **Confident** that this battle is not yours, but the Lord's. You will be **Obedient** to whatever he tells you to do. You will have **Patience** to wait on Him and the **Perseverance** to press on in spite of…because as you wait on Him, your strength will be renewed, and finally you can get **Excited** because, as it was with Joshua, the battle is already fought and the victory is already won.

The Bible says to "be anxious for nothing, but in everything by prayer and supplication with thanksgiving, let your requests be made known to God (*Philippians 4:6*)… and *as you begin to walk around that wall the first time, give thanks that the God of your salvation is also your refuge and your strength, a very present help in trouble (*Psalm 46:1- paraphrased*). *As you walk around the second time, give thanks that you're not walking alone because He walks with you and he talks with you and He assures you that He is yours and you are His, and He has promised never to leave you nor forsake you. *As you walk around the third time, give thanks because you can trust in God wherever and in whatever situation you may be; *on mountains high or on the rolling sea; the billows may roll, but He'll keep your soul, your Heavenly Father watches over you.*[15] *As you walk around the fourth time, give thanks because no matter how bad or how hard the situation seems to be, if you *"ask the Savior to help you, to comfort, strengthen and keep you, He is willing to aid you, and He will carry you through."*[16] *As you walk around the fifth time, give thanks for those inseparable twins—"Goodness and Mercy who follow you all the days of your life." *(Psalm 23:6)* *As you walk around the sixth time, give thanks that "...the weapons of our warfare are not carnal but mighty in God for pulling down strongholds..." (*2 Corinthians 10:4),* and that "no weapon formed against you shall prosper..." (*Isaiah 54:17*). As you walk around the seventh time, get EXCITED, shout the victory and by faith, sing this victory song: "Victory is mine, victory is mine, victory today is mine; I told Satan, get thee behind, victory today is mine."[17]

HEALING FROM A DISTANCE

John 4:46-53 (NKJV)

*⁴⁶ So Jesus came again to Cana of Galilee where He had made the water wine. And there was a certain nobleman whose son was sick at Capernaum. ⁴⁷ When he heard that Jesus had come out of Judea into Galilee, he went to Him and implored Him to come down and heal his son, for he was at the point of death. ⁴⁸ Then Jesus said to him, "Unless you people see signs and wonders, you will by no means believe." ⁴⁹ The nobleman said to Him, "Sir, come down before my child dies!" ⁵⁰ **Jesus said to him, "Go your way; your son lives." So, the man believed the word that Jesus spoke to him, and he went his way.** ⁵¹ And as he was now going down, his servants met him and told him, saying, "Your son lives!" ⁵² Then he inquired of them the hour when he got better. And they said to him, "Yesterday at the seventh hour the fever left him." ⁵³ So the father knew that it was at the same hour in which Jesus said to him, "Your son lives." And he himself believed, and his whole household.*

This was the second recorded miracle Jesus performed. The first miracle happened when He turned water into wine at the wedding in Cana. That miracle demonstrated His power over nature. Now, here He was back in Cana and was sought and found by this nobleman. This nobleman, as the name implies, was not just an ordinary person but rather a high-ranking official attached to Herod in the King's court. He was the King's man and therefore he was a person of great influence, power, and highly likely, great wealth. He probably had just about everything anybody could ever want. Unfortunately, however, there are some things that power, influence, and even money can't get for you. Money can buy a house, but it can't buy a home. Money can buy a bed, but it can't buy a good night's sleep. Money can buy companionship, but it can't buy genuine friendship. Money can buy jewels, but it can't buy joy. Money can buy a good security system for your home such as ASP or ADT, but it can't buy salvation and security for your soul. That was purchased only by JTC (Jesus, the Christ).

This nobleman who had great power and great prestige also had a great problem. He had a son who was extremely sick. The Bible doesn't say this, but in my sanctified imagination, I think that, like the woman with the issue of blood, this nobleman had probably gone to the best physicians, but they couldn't do anything for him. I imagine that being a person of such great means, he had probably exhausted a few other resources looking for some help for his son. You know how we do. When we get those dreaded phone calls, those call backs, if you will, with reports we really didn't want to hear, we begin to look for another way out. We get a second opinion, sometimes a third opinion, hoping that somebody is going to tell us what **we** want to hear....that a mistake was made concerning the first diagnosis; that perhaps there was just a shadow on that ex-ray—that what they thought they saw was not really what they had seen after all. We hope and pray that yet another consultation will tell us that we will not die, but live. I can imagine that it was no different for this nobleman, and he has apparently come to the realization now that all of his power, influence, and wealth are not enough to cure his son, so he's come to find Jesus to ask Him to heal his son.

The Bible says that when this nobleman heard that Jesus had come out of Judea into Cana of Galilee, he went to Jesus and begged him to come and heal his son *(John 4:46 paraphrased)*. **HE HEARD ABOUT JESUS**. What had he possibly heard about Jesus? He may have heard about the first miracle that Jesus had performed when he turned the water into wine *(John 2:1-10)*. He may have heard about Jesus' meeting with Nicodemus, the Pharisee who had come to Jesus by night apparently looking for confirmation from Jesus that He was indeed a teacher come from God. He may have heard about how Jesus had not only confirmed His identification in God, but also counselled Nicodemus with information regarding how he might be able to become part of the Kingdom of God *(John 3:1-12)*. OR...... He may have heard about Jesus' encounter with the Samaritan woman, how Jesus had broken down some barriers—a racial barrier and a gender barrier *(John 4:1-26).* It was unacceptable, first, that a Jew should have any dealings with a Samaritan, and it was just as unacceptable that a man should talk with a woman in a public place. But Jesus did both on this occasion and led this Samaritan woman to become a believer. Whatever this Nobleman had heard about Jesus, it was enough to encourage him to go and seek Jesus out as perhaps another avenue of healing for his son. And so, based on what he had heard, he went to Jesus to ask him to come back with him to heal his son.

It's interesting that in a court of law, "hearsay" is strenuously objected to and is ultimately not allowed. One can only testify to what one has actually seen and knows to be factual. One cannot testify to what he or she has heard from someone else (we've seen enough Perry Mason and Matlock to know how this goes). But in the high court of the Holy Spirit, "hearsay" is not only acceptable, but it is an authentic avenue to the solution of the case. Our Lord and Savior, Jesus, was crucified on an old rugged cross, died, was buried in a borrowed tomb, and then arose from the dead. Since this is the act that brings conviction, conversion, salvation, deliverance, healing, and power, and since this act happened so long ago and none of us were there to see it, "hearsay" is our only recourse, and it is the reliable method of reporting these events for the salvation of humankind and to the Glory of God. The Bible says that "...many of those who **heard** the word believed..."*(Acts (4:4).* When Blind Bartimaeus was sitting by the road begging, and **heard that it was Jesus** passing by, he began to cry out and say, 'Jesus, son of David, have mercy on me'" *(Mark 10:46-52).* When the Centurion, who had a sick servant, **heard about Jesus,** "he sent elders of the Jews to Him pleading with Him to come and heal His servant." *(Luke 7:3 paraphrased).* When the woman with the issue of blood **heard about Jesus,** "she came from behind and touched the border of His garment *(Luke 8:44).*

Yes, the nobleman had heard about Jesus and had heard that Jesus was back in Cana, and…**HE RESPONDED TO WHAT HE HAD HEARD WITH ACTION.** Notice, if you will, just hearing is not all there is to it. In each of these scriptures and including our text, when they heard about Jesus, they followed up by doing something. When the nobleman heard that Jesus was in Cana, he went to Him to plead for healing for His son. He heard and apparently, he believed because he set out to act on what he had heard. The Bible says, "so then faith comes by **hearing** and **hearing** by the word of God...". (*Romans 10:17*).

Now this trip to find Jesus wasn't just around the corner, or just down the street. The distance from Capernaum to Cana was approximately 20-25 miles and probably a day's travel time on foot, and the nobleman had no guarantee that Jesus would still be there when he got there. It's not like he could whip out his cell phone and give Jesus a call or send Him a text message: *"Hey Jesus, I'm over here in Capernaum, and I've got a problem I need to talk to You about. It's gonna take me a minute to get to you. Can You hang out until I get there?"* No, there wasn't any of this kind of convenience or communication, and yet, the nobleman, not sure of exactly what he would find; not really sure that he would even find what he was going to Cana for, set out on his trip to get to Jesus. When the Nobleman got to Cana and saw Jesus, he stated his case and made his request.

Jesus' first response sounded like a **REPRIMAND**. Jesus said, "Unless you people see signs and wonders, you will by no means believe."*(John 4:48)* This bothered me because in reading what I was reading, and with my limited understanding, I couldn't see what the nobleman had said or done to invoke that response from Jesus. In my mind, it sounded like Jesus became disturbed and perturbed at the nobleman's request, and I really couldn't understand why. But further reading and meditation on the text revealed that this is Jesus we're talking about, and whether we like it or not, Jesus is able to look beyond what we say and actually see what we mean. Jesus was in the midst of teaching in the synagogue, and you might say that the Nobleman interrupted him, and Jesus' response (or reprimand, if you will) was not only directed to the Nobleman, but to all those who were under the sound of his voice at that time. And this is one of the things we must remember in our own lives. Jesus knows us better than we know ourselves and he looks beyond the words that come from our mouth and sees the intentions of our heart. This not to say that the nobleman was wrong in his request, but Jesus did include him in this reprimand.

The Message translation of John 4:48 says that Jesus said: "unless *you people are dazzled by a miracle*, you refuse to believe." *The New Living Translation (John 4:48)* puts it this way: "Must I do miraculous signs and wonders before *you people* will believe in me?" Jesus understood clearly that the Galileans idea of faith was totally wrong. He knew that they didn't believe in Him as the Messiah, but only in the signs he had performed elsewhere, and they just want to see Him perform signs again. And when responding to the Nobleman's plea to heal his son, Jesus dealt first with the weightier matter: the matter of their faith. The nobleman and most of the Galileans had a "Milwaukee Faith" – (if you will), a "show me" faith; a "prove it to me" faith. That kind of faith that says: "I'll believe it when I see it." They wanted to see more signs and wonders and miracles before they would believe on Jesus.

The same is true with some of us today. For some reason, many folks can't seem to lean and depend on Jesus just because of who He is. The Bible is replete with Jesus' own declarations of Who He is: For those who don't really believe that Jesus is alive and well, Jesus said that "I am He who lives, and was dead, and behold I am alive forevermore." (*Rev. 1:18*). For those who may be on the fence about the truth of this Christian life, Jesus says: "I am the Way, the Truth, and the Life; no one comes to the Father except through me." (*John 14:6*). For you who may have questions lurking in the back of your mind concerning life after death, Jesus said: "I am the resurrection and the life. He who believes in me, though he may die, he shall live. And whoever lives and believes in me shall never die." (*John 11:25, 26*). Yes, some of us are continually seeking His hand rather than His face looking for signs and wonders that He's real and that He will do just what He says He will do. The Brooklyn Tabernacle Choir sings a song, written by Al Hobbs, which I am sure expresses God's frustration with us sometime and is tantamount to what Jesus was saying to the nobleman and the Galileans…. *"How many times must I prove how much I love you? How many ways must my love for you I show…so you would know just how much I love you.?*[18]

Today, we're not too far removed from the Nobleman and those Galileans. Many of us still want more proof that Jesus still loves us, that He can heal us, that He can deliver us, instead of just taking Him at His word, believing Him, and trusting Him just because of who He is.

Apparently, the Nobleman was undaunted by Jesus' reprimand, and **HE REPEATED HIS REQUEST** that Jesus heal his son, and this time he persisted in asking Jesus to come back with him to Capernaum before his son died. He wasn't put off by the response he got the first time. He didn't let the reprimand deter him from his purpose. Sometimes despite the apparent situation, even in the face of what an answer appears to be, persistence in prayer is the order of the day. No matter what it may feel like or what it may sound like, or what the circumstances seem to be, keep on praying! Be persistent! Don't give up! That seeming negativity is not necessarily a denial; it may just be a delay. Jesus' response, his reprimand of the Nobleman, was not a denial and it wasn't even a delay, but it was just the declaration of a truth that He wanted them to know—the truth that He knew the level of their faith, that it was based on their seeing miracles, and not on Him, the miracle-worker. However, Jesus' reprimand didn't have a negative impact on this situation; conversely, it seemed to have a positive impact for Jesus told the Nobleman, *"Go your way, your son lives,"* *(John 4:50)* and the Bible says that the Nobleman believed the word that Jesus spoke to Him. At this point, he hadn't seen a sign, he hadn't seen a wonder, he hadn't seen any miraculous event, he just believed the word that Jesus spoke.

Jesus speaks to us today through His word and we need to get to the place where we believe His word, not based on any signs or wonders; not based on what we see because things are not always what they seem to be and we can't always believe everything that we see. Not based on what we feel because our feelings are fickle and will fool us if we're not careful. We must believe His word just because He spoke it. He who spoke the word and the heavens, and the earth were created. He who spoke the word and caused day to be day and night to be night. He who spoke the word, and the animal kingdom came into being. He who spoke the Word and plant life became visible. He who spoke the Word and the sun, moon, and the stars were fixed in their silvery sockets. He who merely spoke the Word *(Genesis 1:1-26),* can most certainly speak a word into our lives; a Word that will lift heavy burdens; a Word that will break shackles; a Word that will heal; a Word that will bring deliverance; a Word that will set the captive free; a Word that will save to the uttermost, IF WE WILL JUST BELIEVE!!! . Have you ever considered that one of the reasons we don't see some of the signs and wonders that were manifest in the Bible days is because of unbelief in His Word? We read it; we hear it proclaimed Sunday morning after Sunday morning, and Wednesday night after Wednesday night, but does it really penetrate our minds and permeate our hearts?

Too many of us are still like the Galileans…unable to apply what we hear without an accompanying ocular demonstration of power.

The Nobleman believed, **RECEIVED THE WORD AND IN OBEDIENCE, BEGAN HIS RETURN TRIP.** He didn't question Jesus; he didn't dispute him; he didn't ask for any reassurances. The Bible says, "…the man believed the word that Jesus spoke to him, and he went his way." *(John 4:50)*.

There's a time for persistence, there's a time for asking, seeking, and knocking, and then there's a time to knock it off! There's a time to be still, a time to allow God to speak; a time to hear what God is saying, and then comes the time to obey Him—without question, without a sign or a wonder; without the physical demonstration of a miracle—just get up and obey the word of the Lord.

I readily agree that sometimes when God speaks, we don't always understand His directives, and sometimes what we hear doesn't always make sense to us. We can go all the way back to Genesis when God told Noah to build an Ark to save his family and a few animals from the coming flood, and there was no sign of rain in sight, and because Noah believed God and obeyed, he and his family were saved *(Genesis 6:14-22)*. Again, in Genesis when God told Abraham to take his son, Isaac, and offer him as a burnt offering *(Genesis 22:1-14)*. Who can understand that kind of command, and yet Abraham was obedient, and the result was a rescue for Isaac and a reward for Abraham? You remember the story of Joshua and how God told him to have his people quietly walk around the walls of Jericho once a day for six days, and seven times on the seventh day *(Joshua 6:1-16)* . Strange directives in preparation to do battle and conquer a city, yet because Joshua believed God and was obedient, he got the victory. You remember the story of Gideon and how God told him to weed out certain men in his army thereby reducing his army from 32,000 down to 300 *(Judges 7:1-8)*. Doesn't make sense to us does it? Nevertheless, Gideon obeyed God and was victorious. So, it is here with the Nobleman, Jesus told him to go his way, that his son would live. No visitation, no contact, no laying on of hands, no medicine prescribed—just Jesus' spoken word: *"go your way, your son lives." (John 4:50)*.

The Bible says the man took Jesus at His word and began his return trip back home. And while on the way, his servants met him with the news that his son was alive. And when he asked his servants what time his son got better, they said "…Yesterday at the seventh hour the fever left him." *(John 4:52)* When the Nobleman heard this, he realized it was the exact same time that Jesus had said to him: "…your son lives." *(John 4:50)* HE **WAS REWARDED FOR HIS OBEDIENCE - HIS SON WAS RESTORED.**

The Word of God has power! His Word has creative power just as in the creation of the world. His Word has resurrecting power—the power to raise from the dead as it was with Lazarus when He simply said: "Lazarus come forth." *(John 11:43)* No, we may not see people being raised from the dead, today. All of us human beings have a date with death, and that's a date we will have to keep. However, I guarantee you, that the Word of God has power to resurrect those "dead" situations in our lives. It will restore relationships; it will revitalize whatever seems to be lifeless; and even from a distance, His Word has the power to deliver as it did with the Canaanite Woman whose daughter was demon-possessed *(Mark 7:24-30)*. Jesus spoke the Word of deliverance and back at home, her daughter was healed. From a distance, His word has the power to cleanse as it did with Naaman, when, by way of a messenger, Naaman was told to go and wash in the Jordan River seven times to be cleansed of his leprosy, and he was made clean *(2 Kings 5:1-14- paraphrased)*. The Centurion also understood and believed in the power of His Word, and how that power could work from a distance. You remember the story…the Centurion had a servant who was sick. Jesus said: "I will come and heal him," *(Matthew 8:7)* but he told Jesus: "Lord, I am not worthy that you should come under my roof. But only speak a word and my servant will be healed." *(Matthew 8:8)* And the servant was healed. In this message, from a distance, Jesus' spoken word had the power to heal *(Matthew 8:5-13)*. The Nobleman's son was healed from the moment that Jesus spoke the word of healing.

The power of Jesus' word is the same today as it was yesterday and will be forevermore. Although Jesus does not physically walk among us today, He is sitting at the right hand of the Father, and from a distance He will intervene in our situations and intercede on our behalf. Even from a distance, His Word is no less powerful today than it was yesterday. "God's Word is a lamp unto our feet and a light unto our path" *(Psalm 119:105 - paraphrased)*, and when "we hide His word in our heart, [and obey that Word,] we won't sin against Him,"*(Psalm 119:11 paraphrased)* thus putting us in right relationship with Him. "If *we* abide in Him and His word abides in *us, we* can ask what *we* desire, and it shall be done for *us*" (*John 15:7 – Italics mine*).

A gospel song written by Andrae Crouch that was rather popular a while ago is relative here to encourage dependence on our God and His word: *"Let the church say a-men, let the church say a-men, God has [already] spoken, let the church say amen"*[19]. "…He was wounded for our transgressions, He was bruised for our iniquities, the chastisement for our peace was upon Him and by His stripes we are healed." *(Isaiah 53:5). God has spoken the **word of healing**, so let the church say Amen.* "Because he has set his love upon Me, therefore I will deliver him…" *(Psalm 91:14). God has spoken the **word of deliverance**, so let the church say Amen.* "I will restore to you the years the swarming locusts have eaten," *(Joel 2:25). God has spoken a **word of restoration**, so let the church say Amen.* "Stand fast, therefore, in the liberty by which Christ has made us free, and do not be entangled again with a yoke of bondage." *(Galatians 5:1). God has spoken a **word of liberty**, so let the church say Amen.* "…If you confess with your mouth the Lord Jesus and believe in your heart that God raised Him from the dead, you will be saved." *(Romans 10:9) God has spoken the **word of salvation**, so let the church say Amen.* [So,] Jesus answered and said to them, "Have faith in God. For assuredly, I say to you, whoever says to this mountain, 'Be removed and be cast into the sea,' and does not doubt in his heart, but believes that those things he says will be done, he will have whatever he says. Therefore, I say to you, whatever things you ask when you pray, believe that you receive *them,* and you will have *them." (Mark 11:22-24). God has spoken the **word of faith**, so let the church say Amen.* "Be anxious for nothing but in everything by prayer and supplication with thanksgiving, let your requests be made known to God and the peace of God which surpasses all understanding will guard your hearts and your minds though Christ Jesus." *(Philippians 4:6,7) God has spoken the **word of peace**, so let the church say Amen.* "You will show me the path of life; In Your presence *is* fullness of joy; At Your right hand *are* pleasures forevermore." *(Psalm 16:11) God has spoken the **words of joy and pleasure**, so let the church say Amen.*

Whatever your situation, whatever your circumstance, no matter how you're feeling or how your world is reeling, battle on through the night cause you're going to win the fight; even in the valley or standing at your red sea, continue to say a-men cause your help is on the way[20]. From a distance, the Word of our God still has the power to heal, save, set free and deliver. God has spoken, so let the church say Amen.

TOUCHED BY THE
HAND OF JESUS

Luke 13:10-17 (NKJV)

¹⁰ Now He was teaching in one of the synagogues on the Sabbath. ¹¹ And behold, there was a woman who had a spirit of infirmity eighteen years and was bent over and could in no way raise herself up. ¹² But when Jesus saw her, He called her to Him and said to her, "Woman, you are loosed from your infirmity." ¹³ And He laid His hands on her, and immediately she was made straight, and glorified God. ¹⁴ But the ruler of the synagogue answered with indignation, because Jesus had healed on the Sabbath; and he said to the crowd, "There are six days on which men ought to work; therefore come and be healed on them, and not on the Sabbath day."

¹⁵ The Lord then answered him and said, "Hypocrite! Does not each one of you on the Sabbath lose his ox or donkey from the stall, and lead it away to water it? ¹⁶ So ought not this woman, being a daughter of Abraham, whom Satan has bound--think of it--for eighteen years, be loosed from this bond on the Sabbath?" ¹⁷ And when He said these things, all His adversaries were put to shame; and all the multitude rejoiced for all the glorious things that were done by Him.

This story takes place on the Sabbath, and as was Jesus' custom, He was in the Synagogue teaching. As He was teaching, He noticed a certain woman who was probably having some difficulty trying to make her way to the women's section of the synagogue. In those days, the men and the

47

women had to sit separately in the synagogue—the men on one side and the women on the other. This woman was probably having some difficulty because the text tells us that she was suffering from a spirit of infirmity (an unpleasant condition) that had her bent over, and she had been in that position for some 18 years. The King James Version says she was "bowed together and could in no wise lift up herself." (*Luke 13:11 KJV*)

Being in this physically bent-over condition very likely isn't a very comfortable position, and yet, like anything else, when it seems that one has no choice—if one continues in it long enough—one might get used to it. The Apostle Paul said in *Philippians 4:11* that he had learned in whatever state he was, to be content (*paraphrased*). Although this is somewhat out of context, and yet feasible, it might be said that this woman, after 18 years of this affliction, had learned to be content with her condition and her position. She may have learned to be content with being bent over so that her only clear view was of the ground and the surrounding area. She may have learned to be content with being bent over so that she couldn't really look anyone in the face. She may have learned to be content with being bent over and, after 18 years, had probably adapted quite well to her situation. She could probably identify people by the shadows that fell across her path, by their footsteps and/or their sandal straps. Oh, yes, she had probably learned very well how to live with her infirmity, and now on this Sabbath, as she made her way into the synagogue, Jesus noticed her.

It's good to be noticed by Jesus, especially when you're in a bent-over condition. This woman's condition is representative of the unfortunate troublesome situations that confront some of us. Many of us today find ourselves bent over by the vicissitudes of life. Some people are bent over with the burden of a physical sickness. Some are bent over by the burden of mental illness. Some are bent over by the burden of heavy financial difficulties. Some are bent over by the burden of marital discord and disharmony. Some are bent over by the burdens of disillusionment, despair, helplessness, and hopelessness, and, like the woman in the text, some people have been in these bent-over conditions for a long time—so long, in fact, they may just have become satisfied in and with their condition. I'm reminded of the impotent man who had been sick for 38 years—bound by his impotence for so long, one can't help but wonder if perhaps he hadn't become satisfied, even comfortable in his situation. (*John 5:1-9*) Sometimes people have been in their situations for so long that the condition becomes a way of life. For them it becomes the norm, and so they continue along, day after day, in what they have come to believe are helpless and hopeless situations—situations over which they have no control. However, if someone is in a situation such as this woman experienced, one can be encouraged to know that their situation is not helpless. That bent-over condition is not hopeless, and one can decide to make their way into the presence of Jesus, get His attention, and then watch him work in that situation. In the presence of Jesus is fullness of joy and at His right hand are pleasures forevermore *(Psalm 16:11 - paraphrased)*.

Jesus noticed this woman and He called her over to Him. Not only did He call her, but He touched her. Many New Testament scriptures speak of the compassion that Jesus had for everyone, and He showed this same compassion for this woman. Being bent over as she was, she may not have been able to see the compassion in His eyes, but she could certainly hear the warmth in His voice and feel the tenderness of His touch. It's possible that she may have been a little bit surprised to hear such warmth in a voice that was speaking to her because for many years now she may have encountered some voices that were scornful and full of ridicule. Some people can be cruel and insensitive when someone is different—for whatever reason. The object of their cruelty and insensitivity is either criticized, mocked, and laughed at, and to use today's popular word—bullied—or they're ignored and left alone. It doesn't really matter that they can't help themselves; that inside, they're no different than they used to be. But unfortunately, all some people seem to see is what's showing on the outside, the handicap, the deformity, the difference. For decades, judgments have been passed and erroneous assumptions have been made about "minority groups" in this country based on skin color, hair texture/style, language, and culture. It just seems to be an automatic assumption that anybody not of European American descent is somehow inferior and less than the standard. People who are physically or mentally handicapped are seen as different and unable to render adequate service and are thus discriminated against based solely on their outward appearance. All some people seem to see are the differences, and those differences somehow makes those who are different unworthy of being treated with a little human kindness, respect, dignity, and compassion.

People today who are in their own individual "bent-over" conditions can also relate to this situation for they too are sometimes laughed at, scorned, and bullied, or else ignored and left alone altogether. If you have money problems, your so-called friends no longer want to be around you for fear you might hit them up for a loan. If you have a psychotic or mental illness, folk don't want to be around you because you're acting a little differently now, and they really don't understand, and in some cases, they're actually afraid of you. If you have contagious disease, they don't want to be around you for fear they might become infected. When someone appears to be *different* from what society considers to be the *norm,* that seems to be reason enough for some so-called friends to become rude, scornful, forgetful, and scarce. But not so with Jesus.

In the text of this message, we see that Jesus noticed this woman and he didn't see a "handicapped woman," but a woman with a handicap. In other words, He saw the woman first, and then He acknowledged her infirmity. He didn't see a nuisance—someone just to be ignored and forgotten about. He saw a need—a need that needed to be responded to and addressed immediately. This is one of the differences between Humanity and Divinity. Humanity looks at the outside; Divinity looks at the inside. People see a dirty, raggedy beggar on the street and pass judgment on what appears to be a wasted life. Jesus sees a man or a woman who is hungry, homeless, helpless, and just can't do any better. People see a prostitute and pass judgment on her lifestyle. Jesus sees a young woman who has a serious problem with low self-esteem. People only see the faults. Jesus looks beyond the faults and sees the needs. People only see the problem. Jesus looks beyond the problem and sees the person. People only see a person's color or their culture; Jesus sees no color or culture at all. People look at the condition of a person's body. Jesus looks at the condition of a person's heart.

Jesus saw this woman with a handicap/challenge, and "He called her to Him and said to her, 'Woman, you are loosed from your infirmity.' And He laid His hands on her, and immediately, she was made straight and glorified God." (Luke 13:12,13). This indeed was a miracle, but before we address the miracle, let's take a moment to look at the Miracle-Worker, because in terms of being different, Jesus was about as different as they come. He didn't act like people thought He should act. He did things He should not have done (according to tradition). He didn't behave in the way that the society of His time called the NORM. Oh, He was different and therefore He was talked about and criticized.

The text tells us that Jesus did three things that were out of the ordinary for that time and that culture: (1) He spoke to this woman; (2) He touched this woman; (3) He healed this woman—on the Sabbath. We know that Jesus was a Jew, and Jewish men, in that culture, did not speak to women in public; they didn't touch women in public, and no one was to do any work on the Sabbath. The religious leaders saw healing as work because healing was considered part of a Doctor's profession and to practice one's profession on the Sabbath was prohibited (according to tradition). But thanks be to God, Jesus was not hung up on tradition. He wasn't ritualized or customized. Quite the contrary. He was unorthodox and unprecedented. He was not as concerned about obeying the laws of the land as He was about showing love for everybody. He was not as wrapped up in custom as He was wrapped up in compassion.

Now, He didn't just go around breaking rules for the sake of breaking rules, but he did break down barriers and when certain rules of that culture became barriers to blessings, then he made alterations. Ministering to the masses whenever and wherever it was needed was more important to Jesus than rigid rules, tired traditions, and cold and calculating customs. He broke down **racial barriers** when He went through Samaria. Rather than going out of His way to <u>avoid</u> Samaria (as was the custom for the Jews in that day), He went <u>through</u> Samaria. He broke down **sexual barriers** when He spoke to women in public places, as He did to the woman at the well (*John 4*). He broke down **social barriers** when he associated with tax collectors and publicans and talked with women of ill repute and healed lepers. He broke down **cultural barriers** when He responded to the needs of people regardless of race, creed, color, condition, or the day of the week.

If Jesus had obeyed the rules, that would have been a barrier to this woman's blessing. If he had ignored her because she was a woman and because it was the Sabbath, that would have caused a hindrance to her healing. But that just was not Jesus' M.O. (Modus Operandi). That wasn't His method of operation. Remember He said, "The spirit of the Lord is upon me because He has anointed me to preach gospel to the poor; He has sent me to heal the brokenhearted, to proclaim liberty to the captives and recovery of sight to the blind, To set at liberty those who are oppressed…" *(Luke 4:18)*

Yes, this Miracle-Worker was different and broke down many barriers, and He is the same today as He was yesterday. No, He doesn't physically walk among us today, but He is sitting at the right hand of the Father making intercession for us. And although there are some who have tried to resurrect the barriers that have already been broken down, although there may be some mountains that are hard to climb, and some rivers that seem uncrossable, the Holy Spirit brings to remembrance that God is still concerned and works in things that seem impossible, and He can do what no other power can do. He'll open doors that no man can shut. He'll make a way when it seems like there is no way. He'll make crooked places straight and rough places smooth. In the midst of a storm, He'll speak to the winds and the waves and say "Peace, Be still." (Mark 4:39) In the midst of darkness, He is the Light. During chaos, He'll give unspeakable joy—joy that the world can't give, and the world can't take away. Jesus, the Miracle-Worker still works miracles today.

So now, let's look at the miracle that this Miracle-Worker, Jesus, ministered to the woman in the text. In this process of healing, when Jesus spoke to the woman, my imagination causes me to wonder if, because of her bent-over condition, Jesus himself might have bent over also so that He could look into her face as He spoke to her. That sounds like Jesus— bending down to straighten her up; getting down to where she was to bring her up to where He was. Jesus was not one to look down on anybody, and He won't look down on anybody who's in a similar situation. No matter what your "bent-over" condition may be; no matter how long you've been in that condition, again I say just make your way into His presence and watch Him work on your behalf. One of the reasons some people restrict their own release from the situation that has them in bondage is because they procrastinate. They keep telling themselves that as soon as they get themselves together, they'll come. "Just as soon as I can clean up my act, I'll come." "Just as soon as I break this bad habit, I'll come." "Just as soon as I straighten myself up, I'll come." Unfortunately, some of those habits you just can't break by yourself. Like the woman in the text, you can't get out of that stooped, bent-over condition by yourself. Do you think that woman would have stayed bent-over for 18 years if she could have straightened herself up by herself? I don't think so. Let this lesson be a lesson to you and come on into the presence of Jesus JUST AS YOU ARE! Bent over by your bad habits; bent over under the weight of your non-productive lifestyle; bent over by the winds and waves of adversity—whatever it is, Jesus will bend over to you and meet you right where you are. He'll raise you up; He'll straighten you up; He'll turn you around and plant your feet on solid ground. He'll make your life brand new and He will take care of you if you would just come on into His presence.

At this point, someone might ask the question: "Just how do I come into the presence of Jesus? Are you talking about joining the church? Are you talking about attending church regularly? Yes, church membership and church attendance are part of it, but not all of it. However, it is not just about a public religious exercise of becoming a part of the Body of Christ and attending the local church every Sunday. It's about a personal relationship with Jesus, the Christ, Himself. This personal relationship will bring one into His presence. To develop this personal relationship entails constant and consistent communication. In the context of the text, Jesus simply called the woman, and she made her way into His presence and He communicated directly with her. Today, in the here and now, Jesus is not with us in the flesh, but in the Spirit. He still calls us to Him, and we make our way into His presence through talking to Him in prayer and hearing Him talk to us through reading His Word. And when we do this daily, we'll find that fullness of joy and those pleasures that being in His presence brings.

When we come into His presence, we put ourselves in position to hear Him when He speaks to us. When we come into His presence, we put ourselves in position to be loosed from our bent-over conditions. When we come into His presence, we put ourselves in position to be set free of Satan's bondage and to become a recipient of God's blessings. When we call the roll, we find others who made their way into the presence of Jesus and were blessed by their encounter.

The woman with the issue of blood made her way into the presence of Jesus and was healed of her 12-year infirmity (*Luke 8:40-49*). Jairus made his way into the presence of Jesus on behalf of his daughter, and his daughter was resurrected from death back to life (*Luke 8:41, 42, 49-56*). Blind Bartimaeus made his way into the presence of Jesus, and he was set free from the bondage of blindness (*Mark 10:46-52*). Four friends brought their friend who was paralyzed to Jesus and they had to be a little creative to get him into the presence of Jesus. They had to un-roof the roof (so to speak) in order to accomplish their goal, but they did it, and their friend was not only forgiven of his sins, but was able to rise up and walk (*Mark 2:1-12*).

The woman in this text made her way into the presence of Jesus. Jesus laid His hands on her and immediately she was made straight, and she praised and thanked God. Just for a moment, try to imagine how this woman must have felt. It might not be so easy to put ourselves in her place because we, in our upright position, take so much for granted. We've been able to walk upright, look up whenever we want, look from left to right at will, and we only bend over when we feel like bending over, usually just to pick up something that we've dropped or perhaps to do some exercises. But not so with the woman, and now after 18 years of being in a forced bent-over condition, she was now able to stand straight. After 18 years of not really being blind, but yet unable to see a lot of things that we take for granted, she was now able to look up and see the sun, the moon and the stars; she could feel the warmth of the sun on her face; feel the wind and the rain on her face. Now her family members no longer had to bend down to her, but she could reach up and hug them on their level. Oh, how wonderful she must have felt!

The Bible says that upon being made straight, "she glorified God." *(Luke 13:13)* I don't know what her form of praise was. Maybe she just began to walk around with her eyes up toward heaven and her hands raised saying PRAISE GOD! PRAISE GOD! PRAISE GOD! Or maybe she began to shout from the pure joy of being able to stand straight and tall after being bent over for so long. Or maybe she began to sing a song of praise, something like we might sing today- *"I'm free, praise the Lord, I'm free, I'm no longer bound, no more chains holding me...My soul is resting, it's just a blessing, praise the Lord, Hallelujah, I'm free."*[21] We don't know exactly what her praise was, but if it had been me who had been bent over for 18 years, if it had been me whom Jesus had touched and suddenly I was able to stand up straight, I think I would probably sing this song of praise: *"Shackled by a heavy burden 'neath a load of guilt and shame, then the hand of Jesus touched me, now I am no longer the same. He touched me,*

Oh, He touched me, and oh, the joy that floods my soul; something happened, and now I know He touched me, and He made me whole."[22]

As a final word of encouragement, I invite you to come to Jesus. Just as you are, make your way into His presence. Let Him see you; let Him speak to you; let Him touch you and make you whole. If you're bent over, He'll straighten you up; if you're down, He'll pick you up; if you're bound, He'll free you up; if you're soiled, He'll clean you up; if you're sad, He'll lift you up; if you're sick in your body, He'll heal you; if you're depressed in your mind, He'll give you peace; if you've been broken by the vicissitudes of life, like the Potter and the clay, He'll take the broken pieces of your life and put you back together again. Your personal, intimate relationship with Jesus will bring you into His presence and will enable you to hear His voice. You'll hear Him say: *"The Spirit of the LORD is upon Me, Because He has anointed Me To preach the gospel to the poor; He has sent Me to heal the brokenhearted, To proclaim liberty to the captives And recovery of sight to the blind, To set at liberty those who are oppressed;"(Luke 4:18)* You will hear Him say: *"… I have come that you may have life and that you may have it more abundantly." (John 10:10b.)*

LITTLE BECOMES MUCH IN THE MASTER'S HANDS

❦

Sub-topic: Prepare for Your Blessing Text: 2 kings 4:1-7 (NKJV)

[4:1] A certain woman of the wives of the sons of the prophets cried out to Elisha, saying, "Your servant my husband is dead, and you know that your servant feared the LORD. And the creditor is coming to take my two sons to be his slaves." [2] So Elisha said to her, "What shall I do for you? Tell me, what do you have in the house?" And she said, "Your maidservant has nothing in the house but a jar of oil." [3] Then he said, "Go, borrow vessels from everywhere, from all your neighbors—empty vessels; do not gather just a few. [4] "And when you have come in, you shall shut the door behind you and your sons; then pour it into all those vessels and set aside the full ones." [5] So she went from him and shut the door behind her and her sons, who brought the vessels to her; and she poured it out. [6] Now it came to pass, when the vessels were full, that she said to her son, "Bring me another vessel." And he said to her, "There is not another vessel." So, the oil ceased. [7] Then she came and told the man of God. And he said, "Go, sell the oil and pay your debt; and you and your sons live on the rest."

It's interesting to note that Elisha was a prophet whose ministry was much like that of Jesus. Elisha was a little bit different from his master, Elijah, for Elijah seemed to appear at moments of religious crises and would then disappear into the solitude of the desert. Elisha, on the other hand, much like Jesus, walked daily among the people and took an interest, not only in the great events, but the common everyday occurrences in their lives--their needs, their joys and sorrows, their ups and their downs. Like Jesus, Elisha was moved with compassion when he came upon opportunities for ministry and he used his powers to remove sorrow and bring joy into the lives of ordinary men and women. [23]

The Bible records many miracles that Elisha did and the focus of this message on his confrontation of and assistance to this widow woman is considered to be his fifth miracle. The situation with this widow was really a drastic one indeed. Her human provider and protector had been taken from her through death, and she had been left in debt and didn't have the means to pay that debt.

The Bible doesn't say this, but if I could bring this situation out of its sitz en laden, out of its original setting and momentarily bring it forward into today's setting, I can just imagine that a woman in that situation today would have probably received many threatening phone calls and harassing letters demanding either partial payment or payment in full of the debt. Have you been there? Have you had a time or some times in your life when you got into some financial difficulty and just didn't know what to do? Maybe you missed a house payment or two and the bank threatened foreclosure. Maybe you couldn't pay a couple car notes and the bank or finance company has threatened to repossess your car. If you've ever been in that situation—although today, they can't threaten to take your children—yet I'm sure that you can still relate to this widow in her pain, fear, and frustration. It's never a good feeling to be in what seems to be a destitute situation and having to deal with the threat of possibly losing everything.

The Bible says this widow woman cried out to the prophet Elisha, telling him that her husband, his servant and a good God-fearing man, was dead and that the creditor was coming to take away her two sons to be his slaves. And Elisha responded to her by asking her a question: "What shall I do for you?"(*2 Kings 4:2*)

As we continue to take note of this scripture and how Elisha handled this situation, it becomes apparent that our Brother Elisha was probably not the pastor of the *Shechem Baptist Church there in the Northern Kingdom.* Had that been the case, he would probably have called his finance committee together and made arrangements to get money from the Poor Saints Fund, **OR**, he might have advised the widow to wait until

Sunday and he would see that she was taken care of after the benevolence offering had been received, **OR**, realizing that there was a real urgency to her situation, he might have written her a check from his personal account and at the same time, made a mental note to ask the finance committee for reimbursement to himself. However, Elisha didn't do any of this. He just asked the widow a question. He asked her: "What shall I do for you?" *(2 Kings 4:2)* And then he followed that question with a second question—a question that seemingly shifted the burden of responsibility from himself to the widow; a question designed to cause her to take an inventory; a question that would cause her to take a good look around and see what she had that might enable her to help herself. Elisha asked her: "What do you have in the house?" *(2Kings 4:2)*

Now I suggest to you that sometimes when we get into trouble, before we ask someone else to try to fix our problem for us, we should stop first and take an inventory to see if there is something we can do to help ourselves. We should try to see if there is some resource or resources, no matter how small or insignificant they may appear to be, that we might use to help us better our own situation. Many times, we're so busy looking around for the big dramatic solution, looking for the big windfall, looking and waiting for that proverbial ship to come in, and in reality, the answer or the solution was right there in front of us all the time. Sometimes we're so busy looking for God to speak to us in a big booming voice that we sometimes miss out on our blessing because He's right there speaking in a still small voice, speaking to our spirit, speaking in our mind giving us hope and direction. Sometimes, instead of looking outward, we need to look within, and we just might find some of the answers we might be looking for.

Elisha asked the widow "What do you have in the house?" *(2 Kings 4:2)* On the surface, admittedly, this might seem like a rather pointless question. It's already been established that this poor widow woman is destitute, penniless, deeply in debt and about to lose her sons. And the prophet, the one to whom she went and cried out to for help in her desperate time of need, is asking her "what do you have in the house?" *(2Kings 4:2)* On the surface, the question might seem pointless, but if we take a moment to look beneath the surface and consider who's asking the question, we might develop a different perspective. You see, this wasn't just anybody asking this question. This was the prophet, Elisha, the one appointed by God to succeed Elijah. This was the prophet Elisha, the one who asked for and received a double portion of Elijah's spirit. This was the prophet Elisha, the one who struck the Jordan with Elijah's mantle causing the waters to divide which permitted him to cross over to the other side. This was the prophet Elisha, the one who had already performed miracles in the name of the Lord. And when we stop focusing on the question and look at who was asking the question, we realize that the question was not so pointless as it seemed to be because this prophet Elisha knew something that the widow didn't know. He had some insight that the widow didn't have. And I suggest that this is something we need to understand today. Too often, some of us run to our pastors with our problems, looking for advice and counsel. When he or she gives advice that we either don't like or don't quite understand, then we want to question and sometimes even denigrate his or her advice, actions, ability, and authority. "Who does he think he is?" "Who does she think she is?" "They don't know what I'm going through; they don't know my story; they don't know the real deal." What they don't seem to understand is that the pastor is the one whom God has anointed and appointed to this position of leadership, and by virtue of this divine calling and assignment, he or she knows some things that we don't know; he or she has some insights into some situations that we don't have; he or she is listening to a higher authority whose ways are not our ways and whose thoughts are not our thoughts, and therefore that's who they are--the bishop and caretaker of our souls.

Elisha knew—he didn't just think or suppose or guess—but he knew that "with God all things are possible to him who believes" (*Mark 9:23*). He knew that if this widow woman had some small offering, then as a servant of the Most High God, he could open for her a channel of blessing. He knew that **little becomes much when you place it in the master's hands.**

So, in answer to Elisha's question, the widow replied: "your maidservant has nothing in the house but a jar of oil." Now this widow's answer as recorded in the text reflects a negative connotation. She could have said: "Your maidservant has a jar of oil in the house." But instead she said: "Your maidservant has <u>nothing</u> but a pot of oil...the word NOTHING reflecting a less than positive attitude and indicating that she believed that what she had was insignificant and unimportant so far as her personal problem was concerned. From her perspective, her answer was justified. After all, what good was one jar of oil? It wouldn't pay her debt. It wouldn't satisfy her creditor. It wouldn't keep her from losing her sons. What good was it?

Unfortunately, this kind of perspective seems to invade the faith community today. There are many people who, when asked to render some service for the Lord, respond with that same kind of negativity. "I work all day and I don't have that much time to spare, so I can't go out to Bible Study or prayer service in the middle of the week." "I don't have that much money so I can't tithe and give offerings every time they ask for money." "I don't have but a little bit of education (don't have all those letters behind my name), so I can't teach Sunday School." And over and over we can hear the excuses: "I DON'T HAVE!" "I CAN'T GO!" "I CAN'T DO!" "I DON'T HAVE!" "I CAN'T GO!" "I CAN'T DO!" It's really time out for this constant stinking thinking and negative talking. We need to stop moaning and groaning about what we don't have and start speaking and rejoicing in what we do have regardless of how small it may seem to be to us. If we begin to use what we have as unto the Lord, we'll find that **little becomes much when we place it in the master's hands.** God does not expect you to give according to what others give, but to give according to how He has prospered you. He says: "Bring all the tithes into the storehouse, That there may be food in My house, And try Me now in this," Says the LORD of hosts, "If I will not open for you the windows of heaven And pour out for you *such* blessing That *there will* not *be room enough to receive it." (Malachi 3:10)*. In other words, bring <u>YOUR</u> TITHE, <u>YOUR</u> 10 PERCENT (whether it's $100 or $10 or $1) into the storehouse and see if God won't pour YOU out a blessing that YOU won't have room enough to receive.

You may not have the letters, the BS, MS, or Ph.D. degree behind your name, but you must be showing some sign of intelligence or they wouldn't have asked you to participate, so such as you have, share that with your Sunday School and watch God bless your efforts.

The widow said she had nothing but a jar of oil, and Elisha proceeded to tell her to "go, borrow vessels from everywhere, from all your neighbors— empty vessels; do not gather just a few." *(2 Kings 4:3)* Now with just a jar of oil (and that was probably a small jar), I can imagine that widow probably hesitated for a moment, wondering to herself: "Why is he telling me to go borrow empty pots?" Or to use today's attitude and action: "Seriously?" "For real? I just told you all I've got is this little bit of oil and you want me to go bother my neighbors for their jars? For what? What's the use?"

What's the use? What's the use? That same question might have been asked by Jesus' disciples at the wedding in Cana where Jesus performed his first miracle. What's the use of filling all the big pots with water when the guests wanted more wine (*John 2*)?

What's the use? In effect, this question was asked by one of the disciples when Jesus was making plans to feed the multitude of folk who we're waiting to hear a word from him. They had gone through the crowd and all they could find was one little boy who had a lunch, and Andrew wanted to know what good was the little boy's lunch consisting of two fish and five barley loaves when there were so many people to be fed (*John 6:9*).

Sometimes we hear this same question today. "What's the use? Every time I take one step forward, it seems like I get knocked two steps back. What's the use in trying to continue to get ahead?" "Every time I try to put a little money aside, some emergency comes up and there it goes. What's the use?" "Every time I think my child has straightened herself out and is on the right path, she gets into trouble again. What's the use?" "Every time I think my relationship is getting better, my spouse acts up again. What's the use?" "What's the use in continuing to hope when it seems like all hope is gone?" "What's the use in trying to keep on holding on when it seems like I don't have anything to hold onto?" "What's the use in gathering up a whole lot of empty pots when all I have is just enough oil that probably won't fill up one pot?"

If anybody is asking any of these questions, I'm glad you asked. You've now given me permission to share with you **(1)** ***the principle of making positive preparations amid your present position***. I can tell you about preparing for your blessings even before you know when, where or how your blessing is coming. So often we miss our blessing because we fail to prepare to receive what we've asked for.

The story is told about a little girl who was walking down the street one bright sunny day carrying an umbrella. Someone stopped her and said, Samantha, the sun is shining bright, it's a beautiful day and there's no rain in sight. Why are you carrying your umbrella? Samantha said: "I heard my momma and daddy praying last night. They were reminding God of how dry it's been and how the crops need water. They were asking God to please send the rain. It ain't here yet, but it's gonna rain and I'm gonna be ready when it comes."

Too often, we don't prepare for what we've asked for because we can't see it. We don't prepare ourselves for our blessing because we can't see the blessing. Do you not know, have you not heard that as believers, we are to "walk by faith and not by sight?" (*2 Corinthians 5:7*). Oh, it's easy to prepare for what you've already seen. It's easy to prepare when you have all the facts and the figures, but that's not exercising faith; that's exercising efficiency. However, when you ask for a blessing and then make preparations to receive that blessing sight unseen, that's walking by faith and that kind of faith pleases God; that kind of faith changes things; that kind of faith brings answers to prayers and brings solutions to problems. **That kind of faith makes little become much when you place it in the Master's hands.**

I remember the report that when the disciples were obedient and filled the pots with water at the wedding, the water was changed to wine (*John 2*); I remember the report that more than 5,000 people were fed with those two little fish and five loaves of bread and they still had plenty leftovers (*John 6*). And what God has done for others, God will do the same for you, me, and for everybody.

This is what Elisha knew. Elisha understood the principle of making positive preparation. He told the widow to go borrow the empty pots. He was really telling her to prepare for the blessing that was about to come her way. Then he said to her: "when you have come in, you shall shut the door behind you and your sons; then pour it into all those vessels, and set aside the full ones." (*2 Kings 4:4*) In other words, he was telling her **(2) to *pour out in privacy*.**

The widow's neighbors undoubtedly knew her and her situation and were probably wondering why her boys had come and asked for these empty pots. They may have followed the boys back home just to try to see what was going on. (You know how some neighbors are sometime.... not really trying to help you but trying to help themselves into your business).

This action of shutting the door may have been to keep away the undesirable publicity because this was not for public display. It was to keep out those who would probably laugh at her and ridicule her. This could very well be for we know that even in our society today, there are those who will laugh at us and ridicule us when they don't understand what we're doing or why we're doing it. There are those who laugh at and ridicule faith-healing; those who laugh at and scorn shouting and dancing in the spirit; those who laugh at and undermine speaking in tongues; those who laugh at and just generally make a mockery of laying on of hands and being slain in the spirit, and other activities and events that transpire in the spiritual realm. Yet, I'm reminded that they even laughed at Jesus when he went to raise Jairus' daughter. The Bible says they ridiculed him, and the Bible also says that He put them all outside and proceeded to do what he came to do in private (*Mark 5:39-42 - paraphrased*).

Sometimes we must also pour out our own prayers in privacy, pour out our petitions in privacy, pour out our requests in privacy to receive the blessing God has for us. The Bible gives the report about the hypocrites who love to pray standing in the synagogues and at the corners of the streets that they might be seen of men. However, Jesus said: "But you, when you pray, go into your room, and when you have shut your door, pray to your Father who *is* in the secret *place;* and your Father who sees in secret will reward you openly."(*Matthew 6:6*). Our reward does not come from those who are watching us and our actions publicly, but it comes from the One who watches us privately.

The widow's sons began to bring in the pots, and she began to pour out the little bit of oil into the first pot, and as she poured, something strange began to happen. Miraculously she filled that pot, and then she filled another, and then another, and then another until all the pots her sons had collected were filled to their brims. How did this happen? Where did all the oil come from? In the natural, I don't know. But I do know, I believe, and I accept that by faith and obedience, **little becomes much when you place it in the master's hands.**

Ironically, only after the last pot was filled did the oil run out. In other words, sometimes ***(3) God's provision is proportionate with our preparation***. No preparation, no provision; little preparation, little provision; much preparation, much provision. In this situation, there seemed to be a definite correlation between the amount of oil provided and the number of pots prepared to receive the oil. God's provision was as large as their faith and their willingness to obey.

As it is in the spiritual, so it is in the natural. God's blessings to us are limited only by the provisions we make to receive His blessings. When it seems like our prayer wasn't answered or whatever we asked for didn't come, we might ask ourselves the questions, "did I prepare to receive what I asked for?" "Through the eyes of faith, did I see what I could not see in the natural?" "Did I see God's provision?" "Did I see God's blessing and believe it was on the way?" Sometimes when we don't have food to put on the table, we need to talk to God about it, then after we've had a little talk with Jesus, go ahead and set the table anyway with the expectation that God's provision is on the way. If we don't have enough money to pay our bills, we must talk to God about it, then after we've had a little talk with Jesus, we might go back and check the checkbook again, and look at it with the expectation that God, not the checkbook, but God as Jehovah Jireh and He will provide. No! I'm not saying that one should write any bad checks—any rubber checks. Of course not! I'm just trying to encourage behavior modification. We must stop conforming to the world, become transformed by the renewing of our mind *(Romans 12:1- paraphrased)*, and begin to "walk by faith, not by sigh." *(2 Corinthians 5:7)* The world wants us to continue to speak negativity over our situation, but the word says we can speak those things that be not as though they are *(Romans 4:17 paraphrased)*. To "renew your mind" is to stand, by faith, firm and flat-footed on the promises of God despite what you see. To "renew your mind" is to be confident that "God is able to do exceedingly abundantly above all that we ask or think according to the power that works in us" *(Ephesians 3:20)*. The enemy would have us believe that if we don't see it, we don't have it, but as believers who walk by faith and not by sight, <u>we know</u>, that <u>we know</u>, that <u>we know</u>, that <u>we know</u>, that we are a peculiar people, and we do not operate according to the world but rather according to the word, and last I checked, the word says "And this is the confidence that we have in Him that if we ask anything according to His will, He hears us, and if we know that He hears us whatever we ask, we know that we have the petitions we have asked of Him" *(1 John 5:14, 15)*. No, we may not get what we want, when we want it; it may not come with the snap of a finger or in the twinkling of an eye, but rest assured that whatever we need,

God's got it and He has promised to "… supply all our needs according to His riches in glory by Christ Jesus." (*Philippians 4:19*)

The widow woman was obedient—she did as the prophet told her. She prepared; she *poured out in private*; and God's *provision was plentiful* for her need. The Bible lets us know that she had money to pay off her debt and enough remaining to support her and her sons. The Bible reminds us that God will "…supply all our needs according to His riches in glory," (*Philippians 4:19*) and He is not just a God of "enough," but a God of "more than enough." The hymnwriter, Civilla D. Martin, said it this way: "*Be not dismayed whate'er betide, God will take care of you.*"[24]

PUT FEET ON YOUR FAITH

Mark 5:25-34 (NKJV)

²⁵ Now a certain woman had a flow of blood for twelve years, ²⁶ and had suffered many things from many physicians. She had spent all that she had and was no better, but rather grew worse. ²⁷ When she heard about Jesus, she came behind Him in the crowd and touched His garment. ²⁸ For she said, "If only I may touch His clothes, I shall be made well." ²⁹ Immediately the fountain of her blood was dried up, and she felt in her body that she was healed of the affliction. ³⁰ And Jesus, immediately knowing in Himself that power had gone out of Him, turned around in the crowd and said, "Who touched My clothes?" ³¹ But His disciples said to Him, "You see the multitude thronging You, and You say, Who touched Me?'" ³² And He looked around to see her who had done this thing. ³³ But the woman, fearing and trembling, knowing what had happened to her, came and fell down before Him and told Him the whole truth. ³⁴ And He said to her, "Daughter, your faith has made you well. Go in peace and be healed of your affliction."

As we consider the focal text and the supporting passage of scripture, let us take a moment to look at this woman, herself—at her condition and her circumstances—before we move on to analyze her faith. First, this woman had a sickness, a disorder, if you will. She had what seemed to be an incurable disease, and although it seemed to be incurable, it wasn't necessarily terminal or fatal.

This is one of the many women of the Bible who is not known by name. Commentary says that she was called Veronica and lived in Caesarea Philippi.²⁵ However, the biblical text refers to her only as "a woman with the issue of blood" *(Matthew 9:20; Mark 5:25; Luke 8:43)* This woman was diseased with a female disorder that caused her to bleed constantly, and she had been bleeding for twelve years. Again, commentary on this passage says that this disorder may have been either a menstrual or a uterine condition which made her ritually unclean.[26] Old Testament studies in Leviticus reminds us of the laws regarding this situation. A brief review of Leviticus 15:25-27 reveals this:

[25] *'If a woman has a discharge of blood for many days, other than at the time of her customary impurity, or if it runs beyond her usual time of impurity, all the days of her unclean discharge shall be as the days of her customary impurity. She shall be unclean.*

[26] *Every bed on which she lies all the days of her discharge shall be to her as the bed of her impurity; and whatever she sits on shall be unclean, as the uncleanness of her impurity.*

[27] *Whoever touches those things shall be unclean; he shall wash his clothes and bathe in water and be unclean until evening."*

So, we see that this woman was not only sick (and had been sick for a long time), but she was ritually unclean and highly likely socially outcast. Admittedly, most references to this passage of scripture immediately recall its outcome—her miraculous healing. But have you ever really stopped to consider this woman's condition before her healing? Have you ever stopped to consider what a predicament this twelve-year disorder had put her in? Let's analyze it for a moment: (1) Because of the nature of her disorder, it couldn't be made public without exposing her to shame and contempt. (2) It was a chronic disorder which had lasted twelve years (Ladies greatly understand what the usual 3-5-day experience is like). (3) The disorder was continual. It appears that in all those twelve years, there was no interval where she might have enjoyed a period of good health. (4) Very possibly, her disorder was aggravated by the medicines that had been prescribed for her. The Bible says that "she had suffered many things from many physicians. She had spent all that she had and was no better, but rather grew worse." *(Mark 5:26)* (5) This disorder ruined not only her health, but her finances—the Bible says, "she had spent all that she had…" *(Mark 5:26)*

The woman is now alone, probably no friends, in bad health, and the prognosis is not good. There is no money, no Medicaid, no welfare. And probably, if she had had some other financial aid, she had already been to doctor after doctor and they had failed to help her. Again, I say this is quite a predicament, and when we look at this woman considering today's society, I wonder how some of us would react to this situation. I believe it's safe to say that possibly some women would probably turn their frustration into anger—cursing God, the doctors, and anyone else who happened to be handy. Other women would probably have a king-sized "pity party" questioning God as to why this had to happen to them, and ultimately lapsing into a king-sized depression. Still some other women, feeling that they just can't go on like this any longer, and with no hope of recovery in sight, may seek to take their own lives. But if this woman did get angry about her situation (and she probably did), or if she did become depressed and allowed herself the luxury of self-pity (and she very well may have), it appears that in twelve years, she never got to the point of self-destruction. So, it would seem that despite her disorder, **SHE WAS NOT EASILY DISCOURAGED.**

This woman gives us a real lesson in perseverance—a lesson in how to hold on and hold out—a lesson in how to maintain a positive perspective during a not so positive predicament. She had come to a point of literally having no hope for a cure, no money, no companionship and no fellowship, yet when she heard about Jesus, after all she had been through, she saw yet another glimmer of hope. Her attitude could have been completely negative. She could have thrown her hands up in despair and said "what's the use? Why bother? None of the other doctors could do me any good. They gave me medicine, took my money and all I got was worse." But that was not her attitude. She apparently had not given up yet, and this is another lesson we might learn from this woman. Sometimes, in our situations, we give up too soon. We believe that we've done all that we can do, that we've gone as far as we can go and that we just can't go any further, so we hang it up believing that all hope is gone. Nevertheless, we must remember that as long as there is life, there is hope, and that "…with God, nothing shall be impossible" *(Luke 1:37)*. When this woman heard about Jesus, she saw yet another opportunity, another possibility, another possible chance for a healing, and her hope was renewed.

What had this woman heard about Jesus? Possibly she may have heard reports of some of the miraculous healings that Jesus had done. She may have heard how he healed the man who had an evil spirit and lived in the tombs (*Luke 8:27*). She probably heard the story of the healing of Peter's mother-in-law who had been quite ill with a fever (*Matthew 8:14*). She probably heard how he had healed the man who had leprosy, and this healing would have been of particular interest to her and probably a primary source of her encouragement. A person with leprosy was also in that "unclean" category and was not supposed to be out in the town with other people, but the man with leprosy didn't let that little detail stop him. When he saw Jesus, he came to Him, fell on his face, and said, "Lord, if you are willing, You can make me clean." And Jesus reached out His hand and touched the man and said: "I am willing; be cleansed." (*Matthew 8:3*). If this (and the other reports) is what she heard about Jesus, she may have thought to herself, if this man, Jesus, can make the leper clean, then he can also make me clean. This very well might have been what she heard about Jesus that increased her faith, raised her hopes, strengthened her resolve, gave her a positive attitude, and sent her in pursuit of Jesus. Whatever she heard about Jesus; it was enough to **DEVELOP WITHIN HER A DETERMINATION** to seek healing once again for her disorder.

This is what often happens when one hears about Jesus. Faith is increased for "faith comes by hearing and hearing by the word of God" (*Romans 10:17*). We know that Jesus is the Logos, the Living Word of Almighty God, and hearing of or about Him, not only is faith increased, but determination is strengthened, hope is renewed, and one becomes convinced that all is not lost after all. When we hear about Jesus, the *miracle-worker*, the one who took a little boy's lunch of two little fish and five loaves of bread and fed 5,000 men plus women and children (*John 6*); when we hear about Jesus, the *calmer of stormy seas*, the one who spoke to the winds and the waves and they obeyed His will (*Mark 4:39*); when we hear about Jesus, the *healer*, the one who made the lame walk and the dumb talk; the one who opened blinded eyes and unstopped deaf ears; when we hear about these miracles and healings, we are encouraged because we know that God still works miracles and what He has done in the past, He can and will do the same for us now in the present.

The Bible says, "when she heard about Jesus, she came behind Him in the crowd and touched His garment." (*Mark 5:27*) When she heard about Him, she developed a determination to try to get to Jesus, believing that if she could just touch His clothes, she would be healed. Getting to Jesus in the crowd that was around Him that day was no easy task for the woman. The crowd itself, plus the very nature of her illness and her ritualistic uncleanness, embarrassment and reluctance to break the rules, and to be so bold as to push along with the rest of the crowd, and reluctance to try to get close to Jesus—all of these components could have been deterrents to her determination. However, her faith and her determination were not deterred, and it pushed her along despite her reluctance and embarrassment.

Sometimes in order to get to Jesus, we have to move beyond our own reluctance; we have to move beyond our embarrassment; we may even have to move beyond the stated standard of behavior, after all we cannot "conform to the world, but we must be transformed by the renewal of our mind" (*Romans 12:2 - paraphrased*). We must come out of our comfort zone and push ourselves forward to receive the blessing.

Different renditions or interpretations, if you will, of the woman's act of touching Jesus' clothes have been offered. The one that is most familiar is the one that says "she touched the hem of His garment" (Matthew 9:20) (which is found only in Matthew's account), leading one to possibly believe, on the surface, that this woman may have been crawling on the ground and actually touched the hem of His garment closest to the ground. This would not have been unthinkable. In her illness and her weakened physical state, as well as the crowd all around her, it's very possible she was unable to walk upright and resorted to crawling. On the other hand, others have suggested that she might have touched the hem of the sleeve of His garment, still perhaps giving a picture of her crawling, but reaching up to touch His sleeve. I don't know for sure how she touched Him. I don't know if she crawled on the ground and touched the hem of the foot of His garment or if while in that crawling position, she reached up to touch the hem of the sleeve of His garment, or if she was upright, on her feet and just reached out and touched His clothes, but I do know that in some way, form or fashion, she did touch His clothes, and I know this because the Bible says so. The operative factor here is that it wasn't so much the position of her body when she touched Him, but the condition of her heart. It wasn't even solely about the touching of His clothes. What is important is that her physical act of reaching out toward Jesus demonstrated her faith and that is what had a positive impact and caused her to make a spiritual connection with the source of her healing power.

If we're seeking healing today, if we're seeking direction for our lives, if we're seeking solutions or resolutions to our problems, we've got to learn to reach out and touch Jesus in such a way that readily connects with the source of the power that's going to meet our needs. No, Jesus is not physically walking among us today. He's not physically walking down our street today followed by crowds of people, so we're not going to physically touch Him. But we know that when Jesus left the earth and went back to His Father, He sent us the Holy Spirit, the Paracletos, the Comforter, and by faith, through the power of that same Holy Spirit, we can reach out and touch Him.

The Bible says that "when she heard about Jesus, she came behind Him in the crowd and touched His garment. For she said, 'If only I may touch His clothes, I shall be made well.' Immediately the fountain of her blood was dried up, and she felt in her body that she was healed of the affliction." *(Mark 5:27-29)* The woman believed that if she could just touch His clothes, she would be made whole. **Believe** is the operative word here. The writer of Hebrews says that "without faith, it is impossible to please Him, for he who comes to God must **believe** that He is and that He is a rewarder of those who diligently seek Him. *(Hebrews 11:6)* The woman had faith; she believed that if she could just touch His clothes, she would be healed, and she was indeed rewarded for her faith.

<u>First, she was rewarded with a termination of her twelve-year ordeal.</u> Twelve years of suffering had come to an end. Twelve years of shame and ridicule because of her unclean condition had come to an end. Twelve years of poor health, physicians that didn't or couldn't help, and medications that didn't work had come to an end. All of this had been terminated because of her exercise of faith. This should be encouragement and empowerment to those who may be going through something at this time. No matter what the situation is, no matter how long we've been in the situation, no matter how difficult the situation seems to be, we must never forget—there is hope! It won't be easy; in fact, it might even be difficult, but we must hold on and not give up. We must not let the enemy cause us to fall into depression and ultimate despair. As long as we have breath in our body, there is hope. As long as we can look up and speak up and say: "Father I stretch my hands to Thee, no other help I know"[27]—there is hope. And if we'll dare to keep that hope alive, begin to put feet on our faith and walk in that hope, our help is on the way.

Many people often have difficulty ascribing to this positive faith approach to their situation. They feel that their situation is unique, that they're alone, and no one else can possibly understand what they're going through. They can often be heard challenging the faith-walker with these words: "It's all right for you to talk that faith and hope stuff, but you just don't know my situation; you don't know what I'm going through; you don't know what I've had to deal with." It is true that, for the most part, one doesn't always know or understand the pain of others' trials and tribulations. However, there are those of us who have indeed walked through some deep waters, walked through some dark valleys, and been through the fire. We do know something about difficult and lengthy unpleasant situations. We know that they can be frustrating and depressing, but we also know that our Redeemer lives! We know that "God is able to do exceeding abundantly above all that we ask or think according to the power that works in us"(*Ephesians 3:20*), and we know that if we wait on Him, use that power, exercise our faith, He will renew our strength. By faith, we know that "in all things we are more than conquerors through Jesus Christ who loves us, and that nothing—neither death nor life, nor angels nor principalities nor powers nor things present nor things to come, nor height nor depth, nor any other created thing (or any difficult and lengthy situations) will be able to separate us from the love of God that is in Christ Jesus (*Romans 8:37-39 - paraphrased*).

<u>Secondly, this woman was rewarded with a timely healing.</u> One of the literary characteristics of Mark's gospel is his repeated use of the word "immediately." The King James version says: "straightway;" the New King James version has translated that word "straightway" to "immediately." The Bible says that when she touched His clothes, *immediately* the fountain of her blood was dried up. The sickness that had eluded the doctors and their medicines for twelve years was healed in an instant. What man couldn't do, God could do, reinforcing the fact that man's extremity is God's opportunity.

Now this is not to say that everybody is always healed, and that all healings are immediate as it was with this woman. That just isn't so. The Apostle Paul with the thorn in his flesh is our witness that sometimes we just may have to live with our thorns; we may have to live with some of our disorders and/or some of our problems; that sometimes an affliction may not be healed. Paul prayed three times for the removal of his affliction, but God's answer to him was "My Grace is sufficient for you, for my strength is made perfect in weakness." (*2 Corinthians 12:7-9)* Therefore, we must understand that not all healings happen as this one did for this woman. However, there are some things about this woman's actions and her healing that we might consider. A look at this woman's statement: "If only I may touch His clothes, I shall be made well," *(Mark 5:28)* revealed a positive attitude and a firmness in her declaration. She wasn't wishy-washy, her tone wasn't questioning, and her action—moving forward to make contact ----supported her declaration. What a lesson on faith in action. This woman not only talked her faith, but she walked (or crawled, if you prefer) her faith. She put feet on her faith, and, as she spoke by faith, she was moving toward the object of her faith to receive the rewards of her faith. And she was not disappointed.

A further look at the woman's statement brings attention to the word "If" —this two-letter word that's introducing this conditional clause: "If I can touch His clothes…" Notice that she made the condition, and she put the condition on herself—on what she could do, not on what Jesus could or would do. It's important to note here that, as quiet as it's kept, this is where we sometimes fall short of the mark. Oftentimes in our petitions, we tend to put conditions on Jesus. You know how we talk… *"Lord, if you'll just raise me up, I'll serve you the rest of my life." "Lord, if you'll just help me to get the money I need for this bill, I'll do better at paying my tithes." "Lord, if you'll just bring my child back home, I'll set a better example."* We really cannot condition Jesus. He has already laid out the conditions for us, and His conditions are supported by His promises, "For all the promises of God in Him are Yes, and in Him Amen, to the glory of God through us." *(2 Corinthians 1:20).* Listen as He speaks, and in your own mind, insert, if you will, the "conditional IF."

<u>If</u> you "seek first the kingdom of God and His righteousness, all these things will be added unto you;" (*Matthew 6:33*) <u>If</u> you "give, it will be given to you: good measure, pressed down, shaken together, and running over will be put into your bosom (*Luke 6:38*). "…Whatever things you ask when you pray, (<u>if</u> you) believe that you receive them, you will have them (*Mark 11:24 - paraphrased*), "<u>If</u> you can believe, all things are possible to him who believes." (*Mark 9:23*)

It is not for us to condition Jesus, but to condition ourselves which will put us in position to receive the promises. We can say, like the woman said, If **I** can just reach out and touch Him, **I** know He'll raise me up. If **I** can just reach out and touch Him, **I** know that "My God shall supply all *my* need according to His riches in glory by Christ Jesus" (*Philippians 4:19 – Italics mine*)." If **I** can reach out and touch Him, "no weapon formed against *me* shall prosper" (*Isaiah 54:17- Italics mine*). If **I** can reach out and touch Him, "**I** can do all things through Christ who strengthens me" (*Philippians 4:13*). We must stop putting conditions on Jesus, and instead condition ourselves, put feet on our faith and, with a positive attitude, begin to walk by faith in God and not by what we see.

Finally, not only was this woman rewarded with the termination of **her twelve-year ordeal;** not only was she rewarded with a **timely healing**, but she was rewarded with a **"tell-tale" healing.** What does this mean? "Tell-tale" means that there is evidence of something that has happened, and it can't be hidden. In this case, this woman's healing was obvious. First, it was obvious to her for the Bible says that "immediately, the fountain of her blood dried up and she felt in her body that she was healed of the affliction." *(Mark 5:29)*

This is how it is for us today. Whenever we make a sure connection with Jesus, when we reach out and touch Him by faith, something happens deep down on the inside, and we don't have to guess about it, we don't have to wonder about it. Sometimes we can't explain it, and we may not always understand it, but we know that there is *something within that holds the reins, there's something within that we cannot explain; there's something within that banishes pain*[28] — It picks us up when we're down; it soothes our doubts and it calms our fears; it brings peace that goes beyond our understanding; it gives joy—joy that the world can't give and the world can't take away and it brings healing in the midst of sickness. We can't explain it because all that we know is there is something within.

Not only was her healing obvious to her, it was also obvious to Jesus, her healer. Jesus knew that healing had taken place because immediately, virtue (power) went out of Him. And even though He asked the question, "who touched my clothes?" *(Mark 5:30)* He wasn't so much asking for information, but for her confession and confirmation. He was asking for confession from the woman that she had indeed touched Him, and confirmation that she had been made well. She did confess and confirm because the Bible says that she "came and fell down before Him and told Him the whole truth." *(Mark 5:33)*

When we have reached out and touched Jesus, and when He has blessed us, we too, must be willing, ready and able to come forward, confess and confirm that such a blessing has happened; be willing and ready first, to confess and confirm to Jesus, in prayer: "Yes, Lord, You've healed me!" "Yes, Lord, you've delivered me!" Yes, Lord, You've opened a door and made a way for me!" And not only confess and confirm it but thank Him for it. Secondly, we must be willing to tell it, to share it, for you see, when we've been blessed by God, we've been blessed to be a blessing, and sharing our testimony will be a blessing to others. Just as this woman had heard about Jesus and was moved to reach out to Him, so from our confession and confirmation, others will hear about Jesus and will reach out to touch Him. They will hear and overcome by the blood of the Lamb and by the word of *our* testimony *(Revelation 12:11 - paraphrased)*.

SAVED TO SERVE

Matthew 8:14-15 (NKJV)

14 Now when Jesus had come into Peter's house, He saw his wife's mother lying sick with a fever. 15 So He touched her hand, and the fever left her. And she arose and served them.

Mark 1:29-31(NKJV)

29 Now as soon as they had come out of the synagogue, they entered the house of Simon and Andrew, with James and John. 30 But Simon's wife's mother lay sick with a fever, and they told Him about her at once. 31 So He came and took her by the hand and lifted her up, and immediately the fever left her. And she served them.

Luke 4:38-39 (NKJV)

38 Now He arose from the synagogue and entered Simon's house. But Simon's wife's mother was sick with a high fever, and they made request of Him concerning her. 39 So He stood over her and rebuked the fever, and it left her. And immediately she arose and served them.

All three of the synoptic gospels report this same story. The minute details may differ slightly, but the general thought (theme) is the same: Jesus went to Peter's mother-in-law's house; Peter's mother-in-law was sick; After Jesus arrived, Peter's mother-in-law was healed; And she began to wait on them.

The setting of the text places Jesus in the town of Capernaum, leaving the synagogue and going to Peter's house. Tradition has it that Jesus often stayed at Peter's house when He was in Capernaum. A little later on Matthew's account, we can hear Jesus saying (in reference to Himself) that "the foxes have holes, and birds of the air have nests, but the Son of Man has nowhere to lay His head." *(Matthew 8:20)* By this, Jesus meant that He had no place of His own, no earthly home of His own, and so He took lodging wherever He was invited. When He went to Bethany, He usually stayed with Mary, Martha, and Lazarus. Sometimes He slept on a boat. But in this text, He's on His way to Peter's house. He's not alone on this trip, for going along with Him are Peter and his brother Andrew, and James and John, two more brothers (the two sons of Zebedee). They've left the Synagogue now where Jesus had been teaching, and they were on their way to Peter's house.

It's always good to take Jesus home with you after church. Sometimes on Sunday morning when we're getting ready to go to church, we leave some situations at home that when we walk back into that same situation, if we don't have something or someone to sustain us in that moment, then all the preaching, the teaching, and all the praising and worshipping that we participated in during the church service will be of no effect. Ironically, however, some people don't even take Jesus to church with them in the first place, but they go to church expecting to find or meet Him there. However, if we are sure enough confessing and professing Jesus Christ as Lord and Savior, then we really need to follow the Master Card Slogan and "never leave home without Him." When we have gone to church and worshipped Him and have enjoyed the blessings of His presence and His power, we ought never to leave Him there in church either, nor put Him on the hat rack in the vestibule as some do when they pick up their hat and coat, but rather, keep Him with us and take Him right on home with us.

Unfortunately, there are those folks who, after the worship service, will get right out in the church parking lot and begin to grumble, gossip, and gloat; those who will criticize, chastise, and even castigate. These folks sometimes take Jesus off after service on Sunday and won't put Him back on until time for service the next Sunday. During the week, there's no prayer, no Bible study, no meditation on God and His goodness, and then they wonder why things go wrong during the week. They wonder why they have no power to stand against the wiles of the devil. They wonder why God feels so far away from them. The answer ought to be fairly obvious—if you've left Jesus in church and put Him up on the hat rack in the vestibule, that's where you left the source of your power; that's where you've left your way-maker and your burden-bearer. If you've left Jesus in church up on the hat rack, He hasn't left you, you've removed yourself from His presence. Just think about it for a moment…if you've left Jesus at the church house and chosen to disregard Him for 7 days, 168 hours, 10,080 minutes, you've gotten out of touch with the source of your power, **and 7 days without power will definitely make *one weak*.**

This was not the situation with Peter, Andrew, James, and John. As they left the Synagogue, Jesus was right there in their midst, in their company, on the way to Peter's house. When they reached Peter's house, Matthew records the situation like this (*and this is from the Amplified version of the Bible*): "When Jesus went into Peter's house [in Capernaum], He saw Peter's mother-in-law lying sick in bed with a fever." (*Matthew 8:14 AMP*) Mark says: "Now Simon's mother-in-law was lying sick with a fever;…"(*Mark 1: 30 AMP*) "Luke says: "…Now Simon's mother-in-law was suffering from a high fever…" (*Luke 4:38 AMP*)

Now I don't find any particular significance in the difference in the wording except to note that each writer was relating the event from his own perspective, the general thought being conveyed that Peter's Mother-in-law was sick with a fever. We're not told what kind of fever she had—real high fever, seizure-causing fever, or moderately high fever. William Barclay suggests it might have been a fever stemming from the disease, Malaria.[29] Nevertheless, Peter's mother-in-law was seriously sick.

Our society today might very well be compared with Peter's Mother-in-law. It is also seriously sick with a fever, and in the words of Mark's record, it has been sick for quite some time. In the words of Luke's narrative, we might also say that our society is suffering in the grip of a burning fever. There is a difference, however, between society's sickness and Peter's Mother-in-law's sickness—we know what's causing society's fever. It's the infection and the sickness of sin, the sin that began with Adam and Eve in the Garden of Eden and has been perpetuated by humankind ever since. When we look around at our communities, the sin-sickness is enough to make one physically sick. In this day and time, it seems that folk have come to a point where they believe they have a right to do any and everything they want to do, and no one else has any right to interfere. The philosophy seems to be: "if it looks good—grab it! If it feels good—do it! If it sounds good—say it! Doesn't matter whether it's right or wrong—it's your thing—do what you wanna do!

The First Amendment to the Constitution guarantees freedom of speech, so people use that as justification to say whatever they want to say whenever and wherever they want to say it. Television and movies are prime examples. They began the rating system for movies with PG-13 supposedly being appropriate for children of that age. Some PG-13s I've seen should have been X-rated.

Civil Rights laws guarantee protection against discrimination, and people are now using these laws to justify their living any kind of lifestyle. These are not criticisms of the First Amendment or the Civil Rights Laws, just criticism of the loose interpretation which sometimes allows for humankind's baser instincts to take control. Isn't it ironic that when it suits one's purposes, the laws of the land prevail while the laws of God—the sacred Biblical precepts—are ridiculed and cast aside under the veil of "separation of church and state." Almost every day, new procedures are being set: Abortion is legal. Assisted suicide may become legal. Since we can't seem to clean up the junkies, we give them clean needles so they can continue their dirt but not get dirty. Instead of instilling high moral values in our children by teaching them prevention by means of abstinence, we teach them protection and provide them with condoms. We seem to be dancing to the tune of "if we can't beat them, we might as well join them" and as the result of this falling away from God and this rebellion against God's laws, we see a people today not much unlike Israel during the days of Jeremiah, the prophet—unfaithful, unholy, idolatrous, adulterous, and covetous. We see a nation that is caught in the grip of a raging fever of sin. During the time of Jeremiah, the Lord spoke through the prophet saying: "Why have they provoked me to anger with their carved images—With foreign idols?" "The harvest is past, the summer is ended, and we are not saved! For the hurt of the daughter of my people I am hurt. I am mourning; Astonishment has taken hold of me. Is there no balm in Gilead, Is there no physician there? Why then is there no recovery for the health of the daughter of my people?" *(Jeremiah 8:19b-22)*

Ironically, right here, right now, the behaviors are not very much different from what they were in Jeremiah's day, but thanks be to God, we do have an answer to the question, for there is a Balm in Gilead to make the wounded whole; there is a Balm in Gilead to heal the sin-sick soul,[30] and that Balm has not been confined to Gilead. That "Balm" has come down through 40 and 2 generations—passed through Bethlehem on to Judea—was consecrated in Jordan, was tried and proved in the wilderness, then moved on to Cana, and from town to town, and now, in the text of this message, we find that "Balm" in Capernaum at the bedside of Peter's Mother-in-law. And again, as we continue to observe the perspectives of our synoptic writers, we notice that: Matthews says: "So He touched her hand and the fever left her." *(Matthew 8:14)* Mark says: that "they told Him about her at once. So He came and took her by the hand and lifted her up, and immediately the fever left her." *(Mark 1:29-31)* Luke says: "… they made a request of Him concerning her. So, He stood over her and rebuked the fever and it left her." *(Luke 4: 38, 39)* However, Luke does not say that He touched her. He says that Jesus stood over her and rebuked the fever and it left her."

Please notice a couple things here: First, let's look at Mark's and Luke's account that they (the disciples) spoke to Jesus about Peter's Mother-in-law, and asked Him to do something for her. There's a lesson for us here. As disciples of Christ, we too, have a responsibility to speak to Jesus on behalf of those about whom we are concerned—to bring to His attention those who are in need of healing, in need of salvation, in need of deliverance. We have a responsibility to ask Jesus to do something for those who need to be touched and to be lifted. Although we know that God knows all about the sickness in our society, as His disciples, we still have a responsibility to bring the sickness to His attention. In our prayer time, we must bring to His attention and intercede on behalf of the prostitute on the corner looking for another John; the junkie in the alley looking for another fix; the teen-ager in school with a gun in his locker, condoms in his pocket, and no hope in his heart; the pregnant girl who thinks she has no way out but to kill her unborn baby. This is another reason why it is so important and so necessary to keep Jesus with us and take him with us wherever we go—so that when the opportunities arise for witness and intercession; when there is an urgent need for the application of a soothing salve (that precious Balm), we don't have to run back to the church to look for Jesus. We don't have to reach up and pull Jesus down off the hat rack, but like the disciples, we can speak to Jesus right where we are, and we can immediately intercede on behalf of those who are in need.

The second point I want to lift up here has to do with the perceptions of the writers regarding Peter's Mother-in-law's healing: Matthew reports that "Jesus *touched her hand* and the fever left her;" Mark reports that "Jesus *took her by the hand* and lifted her up and the fever left her;" Luke reports that "Jesus *stood over her, rebuked the fever,* and it left her." Now according to these three, there are slight differences in their perspective of the way her healing came about, but the bottom line is that the fever left her, and she was indeed healed. Whether Jesus touched her hand and lifted her up, or merely spoke to her situation, either way, the Balm, the Soothing Salve, was applied, it's healing properties were released, and the fever left her.

It's so good to know that **CONTACT** with Jesus is the redeeming factor here. Whether you touch Jesus, or Jesus touches you, or if Jesus just speaks to your situation—as long as contact is made—it releases His power—His power to heal, His power to save, His power to deliver. It's like trying to connect a lamp with a short cord to the electrical power source in the wall. You may have to move the lamp closer to the wall socket, or you may have to get an extension cord and extend the power from the wall socket to the lamp, but it really doesn't make much difference which way you do it as long the connection is made—as long as contact is made—the light will come on!

We are reminded of the woman with the issue of blood (*Luke 8:43-49*). She reached out and touched Jesus' clothes and the fountain of her blood dried up. This woman was healed when she touched His clothes. We are reminded of the man who was born blind (*John 9:1-2*). Jesus spat on the ground, made clay of the spittle, and touched the man's eyes then sent him to wash in the pool of Siloam and he came seeing. This man was healed after having been touched by Jesus. We are reminded of the centurion whom Jesus had met just before going to Peter's house, who's servant was at home sick (*Matthew 8:5-9*), and from a distance, Jesus spoke to the situation and the centurion's servant was healed in the same hour.

What He has done for others, He'll do the same for us. What He did so long ago in the flesh, He can do right now in the spirit. We can touch Him through prayer, we can touch Him through His word. He can touch us in the Spirit, or He can just speak a word and work out our situation, whatever it is. Contact with Jesus will bring healing—healing for physical sickness, healing for mental sickness, healing for soul sickness. Contact with Jesus will mend broken relationships. Contact with Jesus will open the eyes of the blind, will make the lame walk and the dumb talk. Contact with Jesus will set the captive free.

But...the story doesn't end with this healing miracle. It doesn't end with Peter's mother-in-law being miraculously and immediately healed. This message was included in this writing because of the miraculous healing of Peter's mother-in-law; however, a more important concept must be shared as we bring this to a conclusion. Listen again to the ending of each writer's report. Matthew says: "...And she arose and served them." *(Matthew 8:15)* Mark says: "...and immediately the fever left her. And she served them." *(Mark 1:31)* Luke says: "...and immediately she arose and served them." *(Luke 4:39)* All three writers agree that once Peter's mother-in-law was healed, she began to serve. The scriptures imply that she served them by attending to their physical needs. Perhaps she prepared a meal; perhaps she prepared for them to spend the night. Whatever it was that she did, she served them, she waited on them; she ministered to them, she attended to their needs.

And so, it must be with all of us who have been saved and set free from the burning fever of sin. We have been saved to serve and we must serve the God of our salvation. The way we serve our God is to serve others and we do that by serving, waiting on, and ministering to others whenever the opportunity presents itself. For a moment, let us look again at the order of events in the text: Peter, Andrew, James, and John left the synagogue and took Jesus with them to Peter's mother-in-law's house. There Peter's mother-in-law was healed. After her healing, she began to serve. We love to come to church, to sit in our pretty (air-conditioned in the summertime and well-heated in the wintertime) sanctuaries. We love to sing and shout, hear the preaching and the teaching, and enjoy the fellowship. But that's just the **WORSHIP** part of our service. After the worship, we must then leave the sanctuary and go to **WORK** for the service begins when the worship ends. We've got to leave the church, take Jesus with us and go where the sickness is; leave the church, take Jesus with us and go and minister to the helpless, the hopeless, and the homeless; the disinherited, the depressed and the downtrodden; the least, the lost and the left-out. We must leave the church, take Jesus with us and with the help of Jesus, put those who are suffering from the fever in the position where they can either touch Jesus or be touched by Jesus. Those of us who have already been through the test have a testimony and we can serve others by testifying of the goodness and mercy of a gracious and merciful God. We can and we must lift up the name of Jesus being mindful that Jesus said: "And I, if I am lifted up from the earth, will draw all peoples to myself" *(John 12:32)*. However, we must not only tell it, for it's really a "show and tell" operation. Jesus said, "Let your light so shine before men that they may see your good works and glorify the Father which is in Heaven *(Matthew 5:16)*. So, we must not only talk the talk, but we must walk the walk; we must not only preach the word but live the word. Don't let what we do contradict what we say, or we will lose before we even begin.

We have much work to do as we bring Jesus to those who need a touch from the Master. And when the contact is made, the fever will subside and they will be able to say, in the words of that old hymn, *"I was shackled by a heavy burden, 'neath a load of guilt and shame; then the hand of Jesus touched me, now I am no longer the same. He touched me, oh, He touched me, and oh, the joy that floods my soul; something happened, and now I know, He touched me, and He made me whole."*[31]

WHEN THE DEMAND IS GREATER THAN THE SUPPLY

Luke 9:10-17(NKJV)

10. When the apostles returned, they reported to Jesus what they had done. Then he took them with him, and they withdrew by themselves to a town called Bethsaida, ¹¹ but the crowds learned about it and followed him. He welcomed them and spoke to them about the kingdom of God and healed those who needed healing. ¹² Late in the afternoon the Twelve came to him and said, "Send the crowd away so they can go to the surrounding villages and countryside and find food and lodging, because we are in a remote place here." ¹³ He replied, "You give them something to eat." They answered, "We have only five loaves of bread and two fish—unless we go and buy food for all this crowd." ¹⁴ (About five thousand men were there.) But he said to his disciples, "Have them sit down in groups of about fifty each." ¹⁵ The disciples did so, and everyone sat down. ¹⁶ Taking the five loaves and the two fish and looking up to heaven, he gave thanks and broke them. Then he gave them to the disciples to distribute to the people. ¹⁷ They all ate and were satisfied, and the disciples picked up twelve basketfuls of broken pieces that were left over.

This pericope of scripture is a report of one of the miracles that Jesus performed during His three-year ministry, and it is the only one of the signs that is recorded by all four gospel writers. Because all the gospel writers don't give the same accounts of these signs, the skeptics, the critics, and the naysayers of the Bible might be inclined to say (concerning this particular sign), that although they don't all tell it exactly the same way, "at least they all agree on something—there was a feeding of 5,000—and they got this one right." Nevertheless, regardless of the skeptics and the critics, regardless of the seeming differences in the gospel accounts, "all Scripture is given by inspiration of God, and is profitable for doctrine, for reproof, for correction and for instruction in righteousness." (*2 Timothy 3:16*)

Most of us, at one time or another have experienced, or at least can relate to, a situation in which it seems like, or feels like the demand is so much greater than the supply. Not enough food to feed the family; not enough funds for the college tuition; not quite enough money to meet the mortgage payment; you just seemed to run out of money before you run out of month. These kinds of situations do not feel good especially when you love and care about your family and their welfare, and you want the absolute best for them. So, what do you do when the resources are inadequate? What do you do when the little you have just won't stretch far enough to make the ends meet?

Some people have been known to become quite creative in their answers to this question, (not going to specifically identify any of these creative activities), but suffice it to say that some people strongly believe in that phrase that is often heard: "by any means necessary" and they have taken it upon themselves to do whatever it takes to try to meet their needs. Sometimes "whatever it takes" has taken them in the wrong direction. The "whatever it takes" has caused them to take a wrong turn. The "whatever it takes" has created a mindset that causes them to make a wrong decision, and they have ultimately created another situation that has only made their lives even more complicated. As believers, we know (or at least we should know) that there is a better way. As believers, by now we should have learned and hidden enough Word in our heart that will sustain us in our times of need. We should have learned by now that God is Jehovah Jireh. He is a provider and that "*He* shall supply all *our* need according to His riches in glory" (*Philippians 4:19 – Italics mine*). By now we should have learned that God is Emanuel, that He is with us and that "…He, Himself has said, 'I will never leave you nor forsake you.'" (*Hebrews 13:5*). Some people have not yet gotten to this place in their journey. Some folk have not reached the level of "what we should know and practice," and are still on the level of "not exactly sure of what to do" and are seriously asking the questions: "What do I do when my needs are greater than what I've got?"

"What do I do when my demand is so much greater than my supply?" For those people, your answer can be found in this message. When you have a large demand, but just a little supply, the first thing you need to do is **LOOK FOR A SOLUTION BY LETTING JESUS KNOW ABOUT THE SITUATION.** One hymn writer said: *"Have a little talk with Jesus; tell Him all about your troubles."*[32] When our needs are more than we can handle, we need to take this situation to Jesus and tell Him all about it.

Our text tells us that the disciples had just returned from a mission that Jesus had sent them out on earlier, and now Jesus was taking them away for a little respite. He took them to a little town near Bethsaida, and although Jesus and the disciples were probably planning on a little quiet time alone, the crowds of people had heard about their hiatus and they followed them, and Jesus, being true to his basic nature of showing compassion, welcomed the people and began to minister to their needs. However, as it began to grow late in the day, the people were getting hungry, and there seemed to be no provisions for the crowd, nothing for them to eat, and no nighttime accommodations. So, the disciples, presumably looking for a solution, took the situation to Jesus, yet, their attitude as they approached Jesus, seemed to leave a little something to be desired. They acted as if they, themselves, had the solution rather than asking Jesus for a solution. They seemed to be telling Jesus what to do. The Bible says that they told Jesus to: "Send the multitude away, that they may go into the surrounding towns and country, and lodge and get provisions; for we are in a deserted place here." *(Luke 9:12)*

Oftentimes, we are also guilty of this same kind of approach to Jesus. We've gone to Jesus with our situations, and instead of asking Jesus what His will is in our situation, we give Him our suggestions and pre-meditated solutions. We present our "grocery list" of needs and wants, and then wait expectantly for His provisions to magically appear. Like the disciples, we could be found guilty of telling Jesus our problem and then telling Him how to handle our problem. God really does not need our help and He's not our cosmic bell boy. He's not that someone for whom we can just snap our fingers and He runs to do our bidding. He's not our personal errand boy who runs and fetches at our command, and then we flip Him a tip for His trouble. However, he does care for us and He's our comforter and our counselor. He's not an errand boy! He's our everlasting portion. He's the one who hears our prayers. He's the one who answers our prayers. He's the one who "…supplies all our needs according to His riches in glory. by Christ Jesus." *(Philippians 4:19)* But although He will answer our prayers, and although He will supply our needs, those answers and supplies sometimes come conditionally.

What are the conditions? Under the condition that we ask…not announce. Under the condition that we let our requests be made known to God…not direct or dictate to God. Under the condition that we ask according to <u>His</u> will, not according to <u>our</u> will. He said: "if we ask anything according to His will, He hears us, and if we know that He hears us, whatever we ask, we know that we have the petitions that we have asked of Him;"*(1 John 5:14, 15)* It's under the condition that we give Him a tithe, not a tip; give Him what's right, not what's left (over). He said: "bring all the tithes into the storehouse that there may be food in My house, and try Me now in this, says the Lord of hosts, if I will not open for you the windows of heaven and pour out for you such blessing that there will not be room enough to receive it." *(Malachi 3:10)*. Jesus is aware of our situations. He knows all about our struggles, nevertheless, it's our responsibility to bring the situation to His attention, with the intention of honestly seeking His will for this situation.

The disciples brought their situation to Jesus, a situation comprised of a multitude of hungry people with no provision for food. The disciples didn't know what to do, but instead of asking Jesus what they should do, they told Jesus what He should do. *"Send the people away to find food and lodging for themselves."* Surprisingly, Jesus had a much different response then they expected. Jesus said, "<u>You give them something to eat.</u>"*(Luke 9:13)* And they said to Jesus: "We have no more than five loaves and two fish, unless we go and buy food for all these people." *(Luke 9:14)*

When one focuses on the less than adequate amount of food they had in their possession, one might wonder why Jesus answered them in this way. As previously stated, this event is reported by all four gospels, and as we look at the reports from the other gospels, particularly John's gospel, we find that John gives a little more detail than did Luke as he reported that Jesus specifically asked Philip "where shall we buy bread that these may eat?" *(John 6:5)* John also said that Jesus asked Philip this question to test him because Jesus, Himself, already knew what He was going to do

(*John 6:6 paraphrased*). Regardless of how the gospel writers reported this conversational exchange, the bottom line is that Jesus already knew what He planned to do. And the answer to the question of "why" was that when Jesus made the statement: "*You give them something to eat,*"(*Luke 9:13*) it carried a twofold purpose: First, Jesus wanted the disciples to realize, that, yes, their meager supply of food—the five loaves and the two fish--were basically inadequate to feed such a crowd of people, and secondly, that since they had come to Him, if they would trust and obey Him, it would be revealed that He, Himself was the ultimate source of the supply; that He, Himself was the solution to the situation, and He would provide.

The disciples told Jesus that the people needed to be fed. Jesus called on the disciples to feed the people. The disciples responded, but unfortunately, they didn't respond by faith, they responded by sight. They responded to what they saw. All they could see was the **great** crowd of people, and the **small** amount of food. All they could see was that the need was far greater than the resources they had. All they could see was that the demand was greater than the supply and they were not sure what they should do.

Interestingly, this situation isn't much different today. We've heard Jesus call on us to do something, and we've responded in a similar fashion. Jesus may have called on you to help feed people physically, perhaps to help in the Food Pantry, or maybe to buy some hungry person on the street a meal, but you responded: "I don't have the time to help in the food pantry, or I only have a little money myself and I can't afford to spend that little bit on someone else." Jesus may have called you to feed the people spiritually, perhaps to teach Sunday School or a Bible class, or just share a Bible study with someone who is seeking to know more about Jesus, but you responded: "I only have a little of education; I don't know very much about the Bible; I can't teach." Jesus may have called on you to feed people socially, (not on social media), but to have face-to-face, up close and personal contact with folk who may be lonely, downhearted, depressed, and sad, but you responded, "I'm not a social worker. I don't have that kind of training or experience. I don't know how to deal with those folks." Like the disciples, you're responding by sight and negativity. You're focusing on what you don't have, and you're failing to take into account that if and when the directive comes from Jesus, then what few resources you do have—just a little bit of time; just a little bit of money, just a little bit of education; just a little bit of experience or even just a little bit of interest in and compassion for your fellowman—just a little bit of whatever you have will become much when you put it in the Master's hands. When you give whatever you have to Jesus, He'll enable and empower you to do what He's called you to do.

The disciples brought the situation to Jesus in search of a solution, and in so doing, they began to **LEARN A SPIRITUAL PRINCIPLE**. By bringing the situation to Jesus in search of a solution, they put themselves in a position to become a part of the solution. Jesus knew precisely what the situation was. He knew how many people were there; He knew the people were hungry; He knew how much food was available; and He also knew just what He would do about it, but He was not going to do it by Himself. The disciples would be an integral part of this sign of provision, and Jesus wanted them to grasp and understand this spiritual principle of small provisions becoming big provisions when you trust and obey the Provider.

We must learn to listen, hear, and obey when Jesus speaks. He knows who we are; He knows what we have; He knows what we don't have; He knows what we can do; He knows what we cannot do. He knows the thoughts he thinks about us; He knows the plans He has for us. He knows whom He's calling into His service and He doesn't always call the equipped, but He equips those whom He calls. So, it would behoove us to pay close attention and be obedient to His calling, and then watch Him equip and empower us for the task. Watch Him enlarge our territory. Watch Him expand our training and watch Him provide the resources to meet the needs.

Jesus not only told the disciples to feed the people, but He told the disciples to have the people sit down, and it's implied in the text that the disciples did as Jesus asked, because in verse 15, we're told that the people sat down. In other words, the disciples **LISTENED TO AND OBEYED THE SPOKEN WORD THEY HEARD FROM JESUS.** When the demands in our life are greater than the supply, when we take the situation to Jesus looking for a solution, we must listen and obey when He gives us direction.

The disciples told the people to sit down and more than 5,000 people were obedient and assembled themselves in an orderly fashion. This part of the story was particularly interesting because the people were obedient and apparently sat down in groups even **before** they had any assurance that they would be fed. At this point, all that was a certainty was that the disciples had in their possession a little boy's lunch which was five loaves of bread and two fish, and I don't believe that this was common knowledge throughout that whole crowd of folk (although, when folk are hungry, I suppose the news of food might spread rather quickly). We don't know what the disciples may have said to the people to encourage them to sit down in an orderly fashion, we just know that they did sit down. You might say that the people rested themselves in anticipation, expectation, and preparation to be fed.

Many times we don't always know where our blessing is coming from, but after we have prayed, it would be in our best interest to rest ourselves—our mind, our nerves, and our spirit in that same sense of anticipation and expectation. Too often, many people, even after praying, waste a lot of time and energy, fussing and fretting, worrying, and vacillating between belief and unbelief as they focus on the circumstances. But the reality is that after prayer, we must allow the Holy Spirit to calm our spirit and help us to prepare ourselves to receive what we've prayed for. And in the process of calming and waiting and resting, we might also want to recall and remember some of the blessings God has already so graciously given us. Remember when the rent was due and you had a light bill, too, and you may have been a little worried, but somehow, they both got paid. Remember when your spouse seemed to have forgotten his or her wedding vows and was now ready to depart even though you weren't dead yet, but somehow God intervened and worked it out. It may not be perfect, but it's better now than it was before. Remember when some of your friends deserted you because you took an unpopular stand on an issue, and this left you feeling alone and forsaken, but late in the midnight hour, God came and turned that thing around, and in your spirit, you heard His words of promise: "I will never leave you nor forsake you." (*Hebrews 13:5*) Just as it was with Abraham, Moses, Joshua, and David, when God promised to be with them in their assignments, so we must remember, that" *it is no secret what God can do; what He's done for others, He'll do for you."*[33] He healed us before, He'll do it again. He picked us up when we were down before, He'll pick us up again. He fought a battle for us before, He'll fight a battle for us again. He opened doors for us before, He'll open doors again. He provided for us before, He'll provide for us again. What God has done for us before, He'll do it again when we trust Him and obey His word.

The disciples brought the situation to Jesus, looking for a solution. In looking for a solution, they learned the spiritual principle that a small provision will become a big provision in the hands of the Provider. They listened to and obeyed His word. This then opened the way for them to LOOK **OUT AND SEE THE SUPPLY MEET THE DEMAND**. The disciples gave the boy's lunch to Jesus, and when everybody was seated, Jesus took the loaves and the fish, and looking up to heaven, He gave thanks and broke the loaves, then gave them to the disciples and the disciples gave them to the people.

We notice that Luke does not tell us what Jesus did with the fish. Mark says, "…and the two fish He divided among them all." (*Mark 6:42*) John says: "…and likewise of the fish, as much as they wanted." (*John 6:11*) Since all four writers agree that they all ate and were satisfied, everybody must have gotten some bread and some fish and were probably able to make a good ol' fish samich (lol). Might not have had any hot sauce to go with it, but they all ate and were satisfied. Five thousand men plus women and children all had enough to eat. The hungry demands of 5,000 plus people were met with an adequate supply of food—enough food such that there was left over enough broken pieces to fill 12 baskets **AFTER** everyone had eaten. And how did this happen? How did this supply meet this demand? There was no magical sleight of hand like you might see at a carnival when the skilled magician waves his hand and begins to pull scarves out of a container and they just keep coming out, nor were there any magical words spoken. Rather, John reports simply that He gave thanks (*John 6:11 paraphrased*). Matthew, Mark, and Luke report that "He looked to Heaven, and blessed the fish and the loaves" (*Matthew 14:19; Mark 6:41; Luke 9:16 – paraphrased*).

I can remember when I was a child, there were seven important phrases that I had to adhere to in our household, or there would be severe consequences: The first one was *"Good morning."* I had to speak when I came downstairs in the morning and entered the room. Next were phrases of respect for my grandparents (and any other older person): *"Yes, ma'am; No ma'am;* Yes *sir; No sir."* And finally, words of courtesy: *"Please"* and *"Thank You."* "Please" and "Thank You" went a long way to ensure that I would receive what I asked for (if it was for me to have at that time). There were a few times I got what I asked for, but I didn't get to keep it because I walked away and didn't say "Thank You" and I had to give it back. Believe me that didn't happen many times. It didn't take me very long to learn the Thornton principle of giving thanks each and every time I received something I wanted.

And so, it is in the spiritual realm. The Bible says Jesus took the five loaves and the two fish, and looking up to heaven, He gave thanks and broke the loaves. We don't know exactly what Jesus' prayer of Thanksgiving was. The Bible doesn't give us that information; it just says, "He gave thanks." But as they say on the news reports nowadays, "HERE'S WHAT WE DO KNOW." Whatever Jesus said, He said with absolute faith in His Father. Whatever Jesus said, He said it with total trust that His Father would do what He asked for. Whatever Jesus said, He said with complete confidence that His Father's will would be done on earth as it is in heaven. Whatever Jesus said, He said it knowing that in His Father's arithmetic, when the loaves and the fish were added, and all doubt and disbelief subtracted, His Father would multiply, divide, and provide, and the supply would meet the demand.

And so, it should be with us as believers. Whenever we have a situation and we think that the little supply that we have isn't enough to meet the demands or the obligations that we have, take that situation to Jesus in search of a solution; learn the spiritual principle that our small provision will become large provisions in the hands of the Provider, but above all, don't forget to give thanks, and as you give thanks, do it by faith with no doubting; do it with complete trust that He will direct your path. Do it with the confidence that His resources will meet all your needs. More month left than there is money? Take it to Jesus and by faith, thank the Father that He has promised "to open the windows of heaven and pour you out a blessing you won't have room enough to receive." (*Malachi 3:10 – paraphrased*) Sickness in your body? Take it to Jesus and by faith, thank the Father that He is still able to heal all your diseases. Trouble in your home? Trouble in your marriage? Trouble with your children? Take the situation to Jesus and by faith, thank the Father that He will deliver you from your distress in your time of trouble; thank Him that He invites you to cast all your care on Him because He cares for you (*1 Peter 5:7 - paraphrased*).

When your way gets dark and drear and you can't seem to see your way clear, take the situation to Jesus, and by faith, thank the Father that "He is your light and your salvation" (*Psalm 27:1 – paraphrased*), thank Him for His word because "His word is a lamp unto your feet and a light unto your pathway" (*Psalm 119:105 – paraphrased*). When friends and sometimes even family members turn their back on you and you're feeling alone and lonely, take it to Jesus and thank the Father for His promise "to never leave you nor forsake you" (*Hebrews 13:5 – paraphrased*).

I cannot promise that there will be an instant, miraculous response as it was with this sign/miracle of the loaves and the fishes, but if you trust and believe, you can have the blessed assurance that the Father **will** answer, and in His time and in His way, He **will** supply all your needs according to His riches in glory by Christ Jesus (*Philippians 4:13 – paraphrased*). In His time and in His way, when you add to your faith, trust, and belief, then subtract your doubt, fears, and unbelief, He will multiply, divide, and provide. The old folks used to say, "He may not come when you want Him, but when He does come, He comes on time." Whatever your situation, whatever your trial, trouble or tribulation, whatever your problem, whatever circumstances are confronting you, whenever the demands seem to be greater than your supply, "*have a little talk with Jesus, tell Him all about your troubles, He'll hear your faintest cry and He'll answer bye and bye. When you feel the prayer wheel turning, you'll know the fire is burning and you'll find a little talk with Jesus will make everything all right.*"[34]

TAKE TIME TO SAY "THANK YOU"

Luke 17:11-19 (NKJV)

¹¹ Now it happened as He went to Jerusalem that He passed through the midst of Samaria and Galilee. ¹² Then as He entered a certain village, there met Him ten men who were lepers, who stood afar off. ¹³ And they lifted up their voices and said, "Jesus, Master, have mercy on us!" ¹⁴ So when He saw them, He said to them, "Go, show yourselves to the priests." And so, it was that as they went, they were cleansed. ¹⁵ And one of them, when he saw that he was healed, returned, and with a loud voice glorified God, ¹⁶ and fell down on his face at His feet, giving Him thanks. And he was a Samaritan. ¹⁷ So Jesus answered and said, "Were there not ten cleansed? But where are the nine? ¹⁸ Were there not any found who returned to give glory to God except this foreigner?" ¹⁹ And He said to him, "Arise, go your way. Your faith has made you well."

This text tells the story of ten men, nine (9) Jews and one (1) Samaritan, all of whom were afflicted with one of the most terrible diseases imaginable at that time. A disease so terrible and so contagious that those who were afflicted, according to Jewish law, had to be separated from family and friends and confined outside of the camp. They were to stay away from other folk, and if they did happen to encounter other people, again, according to Jewish law, they were to cover the lower part of their faces and shout "Unclean, Unclean" so that others would know they were there and not go near them *(Read Leviticus chapters 13, 14)*.

Now there's an interesting fact in this story that needs to be shared, and that is that under regular conditions, Jews and Samaritans would not have been found together. There was no love lost between these two races of people and this was because the Jews saw themselves as pure descendants of Abraham, while the Samaritans were a mixed race produced when Jews from the northern kingdom intermarried with other people after Israel's exile.[35] But here in this text, we see that illness and disease knows no race and is no respecter of persons. This band of ten lepers included one Samaritan and he was probably no more or no less leprous than the nine Jews. These ten men, despite their ethnic differences were now bound together by their common affliction. They were bound together by their common need for mercy. They were bound together by an apparent common belief that Jesus would be their help in the time of trouble, for they called on him for mercy.

The Bible reports that Jesus is on his way to Jerusalem and he's traveling along the border between Samaria and Galilee, and as he goes into a village, he's met by these ten men who have leprosy. They were careful to stay off at a distance as they were supposed to, and I don't know if they called out "Unclean, Unclean" as they were supposed to, but I do know that they called out to Jesus, saying "Master, have mercy on us." And Jesus, in response, with no questions asked, no recriminations, no hesitation or reluctance, said to them: "Go show yourselves to the priests." (*Luke 17:14*) Again, according to Jewish law, showing oneself to the priest suggested that one's leprosy was healed or perhaps had gone into remission, and the priest would have to make the determination as to whether they were clean or not.[36]

Apparently all ten men obeyed Jesus and began their journey to show themselves to the priest. The Bible says that "...as they went, they were cleansed of their leprosy." (*Luke 17:14*) The phrase "as they went, they were cleansed" arrested my attention. As they were walking along, probably in conversation; as they were on their way—not there yet, but on their way; as they were headed toward their miracle, they were cleansed. Sometimes, when we ask God to do something for us, we don't always have to wait a long time before He answers and/or provides that for which we have asked. God says in Isaiah 65:24 "...before they call, I will answer; And while they are still speaking, I will hear." We don't always have to wait until we get where we are going to realize that God has already gone and got what we needed.

As those men with leprosy were on their way, they were cleansed. However, "…one of them, when he saw that he was healed, returned, and with a loud voice glorified God, and fell down on his face at His feet, giving Him thanks." (Luke 17:15, 16) Only one out of the ten returned to give thanks—and he was a Samaritan; a Samaritan who was used to being ostracized and set apart from the Jews because of his <u>ancestry</u>; a Samaritan who was subsequently brought together with these Jews because of his <u>affliction</u>; a Samaritan who is now set apart again because of his show of <u>appreciation</u>.

Isn't it interesting to note that: they all <u>reached</u> out to Jesus; that they all <u>responded</u> to Jesus in obedience to His directive; that they all <u>regained</u> their health, but only one <u>returned</u> to give thanks. Only one out of the ten acknowledged his blessing; only one of the ten thought it not robbery to show some gratitude for his blessing. And don't think for a moment that the ingratitude of the nine went unnoticed by Jesus, because although He didn't ask any questions when they called for mercy, He does ask some questions now. "Were there not ten cleansed? But where are the nine? Were there not any found who returned to give glory to God except for this foreigner?" (*Luke 17:17,18*)

I wonder if some of us really think that God doesn't notice our ingratitude, our thanklessness, our non-responsiveness to His Grace and His mercy? What a sad commentary, not only on the nine who were healed, but on humankind. When we look around at our society today, we're not much better now than they were then. In so many instances, we seem to be living in an ungrateful and a thankless society. I'm not just talking now about the disrespect and ingratitude we see demonstrated in some of our children. A child's lack of ingratitude reflects his or her parents' lack of teaching and training (that's material for a whole new sermon). But I'm talking about the adults and their lack of thankfulness, or should I say their failure to demonstrate or show their thankfulness, not only to God, but to each other. And I emphasize "demonstrate or show thankfulness" because some people will say: "What are you talking about, preacher? I'm thankful." In my heart, I'm thankful! In my mind, I'm thankful! But I must reply, "if you don't show it, people won't know it, and they cannot be expected to read your heart or your mind." The Samaritan <u>demonstrated</u> his gratitude. He showed his gratitude. He showed his thankfulness for his healing by taking the time to go back, give God the glory, fall at Jesus' feet, and thank Him for his healing.

This concept of "thankfulness" greatly reminds me of my childhood. I was raised by grandparents who believed that "Yes ma'am", "No ma'am"; "Yes sir", "No sir", "Please" and "Thank you" were the most important words in the English language, and to not say any of these words (especially if you had been taught that this was the proper response), was cause for a strong method of discipline. It seems that somewhere along the line today, people have either forgotten or have never been taught the importance of saying "Thank You". A sincere "Thank You" shows appreciation and sometimes means much more than giving money or giving gifts. And when you take the time to show that appreciation, people will be more inclined to do for you in the future. However, by the same token, to not say "Thank You" shows a lack of appreciation. It shows a lack of respect for those who have done something for you and will often cause hurt feelings and deep resentment; and I might add, folk are not so anxious to do anything for you the next time.

This message talks about nine such persons who did not take the time to say "Thank You" to Jesus, to show some appreciation for His taking the time to be a blessing to them. They didn't take the time to say "Thank You" to Jesus for His taking the time to do something wonderful for them. And this healing—to be healed of this dreadful disease of leprosy—was indeed a wonderful thing. It was miraculous, it was marvelous, it was phenomenal, it was extraordinary, and it was worthy of everybody's praise, not just the Samaritan.

I've read this text many times and I've often wondered why none of the other men who were healed showed gratitude or at least said "Thank You" for being healed As I pondered the question this time in preparing this message, to try to make a point here, I began to think in terms of what some of the excuses would be that some people might use today. That gave me a little insight, and in my imagination, I think one or two of the men who were healed didn't go back to say "Thank You" because of **SKEPTICISM**. They wanted to wait a while to see if the healing was real, and to see if it would last. After all, nobody examined them; nobody took their temperatures; nobody gave them any medication; nobody wrapped their diseased limbs in some kind of medicated poultice. Jesus didn't even lay his hands on them. Admittedly, they weren't supposed to be touched, but this was Jesus—He could have at least waved His hand over them. But He didn't even do that, He just told them to go and show themselves to the priest. How could they be sure this healing was real. How could they be sure that tomorrow they wouldn't be leprous all over again?

Many people are skeptical like that about some things, and they find it difficult to believe in things that don't happen according to protocol. They don't believe in miracles, they don't believe in things that happen out of the ordinary, and so they're reluctant to accept strange and unusual happenings at face value. They're not sure that the healing is real; they're not sure that the cancer is gone. They don't believe they can get out of the boat and walk on water. They've not yet learned the principle of walking by faith and not by sight. And so, they wonder: Is this healing real? Will it last?

I imagine that another one of the men who was healed didn't want to take the time to say "Thank You" because of **PROCRASTINATION**. He would go back to see Jesus later, but he had some other things he wanted to do first. He wanted to go and tell his family about the healing. How many times have we received a wonderful blessing, and instead of immediately calling up heaven to thank God for what He's done, we call up our family, we call up our neighbors, we call up our friends, we'll call up the pastor, and sometimes if we want to rub salt into a wound, we might even call up an enemy or two just to let them know that "I'm blessed, and you ain't. How do you like me now?" And then, if we happen to remember and have any time left over, we'll give God a quick "Thanks, Lord" on our way to dreamland.

In my imagination, I think a couple more men who were healed probably didn't go back to say "Thank You" because of **SELF-DIAGNOSIS**. They decided among themselves, that they really didn't have leprosy after all. It wasn't as bad as they thought it was, and whatever the problem was, it was gone now and was probably going to go away soon anyway. Didn't nothing so great happen here. I don't have to go back to Jesus, and I don't have to go to the priest either.

Another man who was healed may not have gone back to say "Thank

You" because of **<u>SELF-RIGHTEOUS OBEDIENCE</u>**. In his mind, he was being obedient. Jesus had told them to go show themselves to the priest, and since he was healed before he got to the priest, he was still on his way to see the priest. No time to stop, now, he had to get to the priest because Jesus said so. Kind of like the other story of the "Good Samaritan in which the Priest in that story was all about attending to his duty at the temple rather than attending to the needs of the traveler who had been beaten and left for dead, and so he passed by on the other side and continued on to the Temple to fulfill his duty *(Luke 10:25-37)*. Perhaps this man who had been healed of the leprosy might have been so busy being obedient, going on his way to see the priest that he couldn't take the time to say "Thank You" to the One who had healed him.

Another man who was healed might not have gone back to say "Thank You" because of **<u>CYNICISM.</u>** In his mind, he felt that Jesus hadn't really done anything so spectacular—that any other rabbi could have done the same thing. Truth be told, there are people today who don't give God the credit for their blessings. They believe that their other resources are the contributing factors to their success. Their education, their money, their family, their status, their position, their doctors—these are the resources that determine their health, their wealth, and their general welfare. They fail to realize that God, the Father is the main source of all resources, and without Him, they would have nothing at all. And ironically, although they don't give God His due credit when they are blessed, they will give Him all the blame when they are broke, beat down, busted, and disgusted. They will only talk to Him on an "as needed" basis when everything is all right, but then they'll pray every day when things are going wrong, and most likely the prayer sounds something like this: "Why me, Lord? God, why did you let this happen to me? Oh, God, where were you when I needed You?"

As previously stated, these excuses that these men **<u>may</u>** have made are only in my imagination, they're not in the Bible, but unfortunately, they are a reality in the lives of some people today. So often, just like the nine, when God does something wonderful for us, we miss it. We make excuses; we **<u>procrastinate</u>**, we **<u>pontificate</u>**, we **<u>discriminate</u>**, we **<u>deliberate,</u>** but we fail to **<u>demonstrate</u>** an attitude of gratitude for what He's done for us. In the text, only the Samaritan seemed to have full awareness and realization of the actual source of his blessing. Only the Samaritan took the time to go back to that source and say, "thank you."

Too often, the immediate provisions for blessings received is confused with the primary source from which the blessings come. What does this mean? Let me explain. Yes, our education, completed application and intelligent presentation of ourselves at the interview may empower us to land employment positions, but God is the source of those employment blessings. For those who are already employed, that job is the immediate provision of your paycheck, but God is the real source of that financial blessing, and your job is where He dropped off your paycheck. Your savings accounts, bank loans, 401ks, and Deferred Compensation plans, provide you the means to make house purchases and car purchases, to send your children off to college, and subsequently allows you to retire in style, but God and His amazing Grace is the main source of these material blessings. Hospitals, doctors, nurses, and other medical technicians diagnose our conditions and help us to recover from illnesses and diseases, but just as it was with those sick with leprosy, God and His tender mercy is the real source of our healing, and we must never forget where our blessings come from. We must always be cognizant of the fact that our help—whatever kind of help it is, comes from the Lord; our help—whenever we need that help, comes from the Lord; our help—in whatever way we need that help, comes from the Lord. All our help comes from the Lord.

Finally, I want to bring to our attention another miracle that Jesus did—a miracle that He has done on our behalf. May I bring to remembrance that one day, we were like the ten men who had leprosy. We were afflicted with the disease of sin which is much like leprosy. It's a nasty disease; a contagious disease, and we were contaminated with this disease. It separated us from the family of God and kept us confined outside of the camp of salvation. But one day our situation became such that we began to realize that, like the men who had leprosy, we needed somebody to have mercy on us. For somebody, it might have been a serious physical illness and they realized that they might not live any longer, but they really weren't ready to die. For someone else it might have been the loss of a loved one. For someone else it might have been a tragic accident that landed them at death's door, but somehow, miraculously, they were snatched back from that sudden death and given another chance. For still some others it may not have been a traumatic experience, but just a sudden reality check prompted by the Holy Spirit that it was the time for a change—it was time to stop wandering in the wilderness; it was time to stop living outside the camp; it was time to stop covering up; it was time to stop figuratively crying out "Unclean, Unclean," and time to call on the Lord—"Jesus, Master, Have mercy on me." Whatever the reason, one day, *we came to Jesus, just as we were, weary, worn, and sad, and we found in Him a resting place, and He has made us glad*[37]. When we called on Him, He heard our despairing cry, and from the waters of sin, He lifted us; from outside the camp, He brought us in. By the shedding of His blood, He cleansed us from our sin and made us white as snow. That was a miracle! He didn't have to send us to show ourselves to the priest because He is our high priest and He has made the determination that we have been healed, delivered, and set free. That's a miracle! We're no longer confined outside of the camp, and instead of crying out the "Unclean" warning, we can sing the victory song: *I've found a friend who is all to me; His love is ever true; I love to tell how He lifted me, and what His grace can do for you .I'm saved, by his power divine; saved to new life sublime; Life now is sweet and my joy is complete, for I'm saved, saved, saved!!*[38]

Like the Samaritan, we must take time to say, "Thank You." We must give Him all the glory, all the honor and all the praise. We, too, must *thank Him for saving our soul; thank Him making us whole; thank Him for giving to us, His great salvation, full and free.*[39] However, our thanksgiving just must not stop with our salvation, because even when we weren't saved, He was blessing us, we just didn't have sense enough to realize how much we were blessed, and now since we've been saved, He keeps right on doing great things for us whereof we should be so glad.

I can't speak for others, but sometimes, when I think of His goodness and all that He's done for me, in my own vocabulary, I feel like I just don't have the words to thank Him enough, but this is what is exceptional about the Word of God. When necessary, I can pray God's Word back to Him, and be assured that He will hear and be pleased with my praise. I can thank Him for being my shepherd. I can thank Him for being my light and my salvation. I can thank Him for being my refuge and my fortress. I can thank Him for being the source of my strength and the strength of my life. I can thank Him for being a very present help in the time of trouble, because in the time of trouble, He's my hiding place—He hides me in His pavilion—in the secret of His tabernacle.

Let us not just wait for the season of Thanksgiving, the season that the world has designated as the time of thanksgiving—the last Thursday in November—to give thanks. We as Christian believers, know that for us, **EVERY DAY** is a day of Thanksgiving, and if some of you haven't gotten to that place yet where you express your thankfulness <u>daily</u> for God's <u>daily</u> blessings, then may I suggest that you try to get there starting today, and from now, hence forth and forevermore, don't ever let another day pass that you don't **take time to say Thank You**!

WHEN THE ANSWER IS "NO"

2 Corinthians 12:7-10 (NKJV)

⁷ And lest I should be exalted above measure by the abundance of the revelations, a thorn in the flesh was given to me, a messenger of Satan to buffet me, lest I be exalted above measure. ⁸ Concerning this thing I pleaded with the Lord three times that it might depart from me. ⁹ And He said to me, "My grace is sufficient for you, for My strength is made perfect in weakness." Therefore, most gladly I will rather boast in my infirmities, that the power of Christ may rest upon me. ¹⁰ Therefore I take pleasure in infirmities, in reproaches, in needs, in persecutions, in distresses, for Christ's sake. For when I am weak, then I am strong.

In the faith community, we are taught that prayer is our way of communicating with God; it's our way of making our requests known to God; and we are taught, through scripture, to believe that God answers our prayers and responds to our requests. The Bible is replete with promises for our every need, and we are told that if we pray those promises, God will answer those prayers. Hear the words of scripture:

(1) John 15:7 *"If you abide in Me, and My words abide in you, you will ask what you desire, and it shall be done for you".*

(2) Matthew 6:33 *"But seek first the kingdom of God and His righteousness, and all these things shall be added to you."*

(3) Matthew 7:7-8 *"Ask, and it will be given to you; seek, and you will find; knock, and it will be opened to you For everyone who asks receives, and he who seeks finds, and to him who knocks it will be opened.*

(4) Mark 11:24 *"Therefore I say to you, whatever things you ask when you pray, believe that you receive them, and you will have them".*

(5) 1 John 5:14, 15 *"Now this is the confidence that we have in Him, that if we ask anything according to His will, He hears us. And if we know that He hears us, whatever we ask, we know that we have the petitions that we have asked of Him."*

(6) Psalm 37:4 *"Delight yourself also in the Lord and He will give you the desires of your heart."*

The list is long, and as I said, the Bible is full of promises that give us hope and reasons to believe that our prayers will be answered as we desire. Nevertheless, a closer look at some of the promises reveals either a definite or an implied condition. There is a little two-letter word that sometimes puts a condition on our prayers and lets us know that along with the promises God has made, we also have a responsibility; that if we are to be a recipient of the promise, we must also be a participant in the process. That little two-letter conditional word is **IF**. If we ask… **If** we believe… **If** we trust… **If** we have faith… **If** we abide in Him… and **If** His word abides in us… **If** we seek Him first… God will answer our prayer.

Not only is there this ***condition,*** but there is also a ***caution*** to be considered as well: Yes, God does answer our prayers, but even when the conditions are met, He doesn't always answer the way we want Him to. He doesn't always give us what we asked for, the way we asked for it, and on our time schedule. He doesn't always give us what we think we want; he doesn't even always give us what we think we need, because the truth of the matter is that we don't always know what we need. Yes, God answers our prayers, but the answer isn't always YES to whatever we ask.

It has been said that there may be three answers given to our prayers, according to His will: YES, NO and WAIT. Sometimes, because of His divine wisdom and knowledge, the answer is WAIT, or the answer may be

NO, and then sometimes because of His divine grace and favor, mercifully, the answer is YES. And because God's ways are not our ways, His thoughts are not our thoughts, and His timing is not our timing, we have no guarantees of just how God is going to bless us. There is no algebraic formula and no geometric calculation that will guarantee the how or when God will answer our prayers. Although we may not understand at the time, an answer of **NO** is sometimes a blessing, for it may keep us from getting things that we really don't need or getting into situations that we really aren't ready for. An answer of **WAIT may** also be a blessing. The Psalmist David said: "WAIT on the Lord; be of good courage and He shall strengthen your heart." (*Psalm 27:14*) The prophet Isaiah said: "But those who wait on the Lord Shall renew their strength; They shall mount up with wings as eagles, they shall run and not be weary, they shall walk and not faint." (*Isaiah 40:31*) Thus, even in the waiting process, there are blessings of strength and support.

No, we don't know when those seemingly negative responses will manifest themselves as blessings in our lives, and while there are no guarantees of how the blessings will come, we still have God's permission to ASK, SEEK, and KNOCK, (and to keep on asking, seeking, and knocking), and we have His promise that, in His time, and in His way, we will receive, we will find, and doors will be opened (*Matthew 7:7, 8 - paraphrased*).

We may receive NO answers to our requests for different reasons. We may receive a NO answer because we, ourselves, don't ask for the right reason. In the book of James, we are told that oftentimes, people ask and do not receive because they ask amiss that they may spend it on their own pleasures (*James 4:3 - paraphrased*). They ask with wrong motives and with the wrong intentions. We may receive a NO answer because hearts aren't right in in the sight of God. In the book of Psalms, we're told that "if we regard iniquity (iniquity is evilness, sinfulness, wickedness, unrighteousness) in our heart, God will not hear us" (*Psalm 66:18 - paraphrased*). Then, we may receive a NO answer, not because of anything that we have or have not done, but just because it's Divine Providence, and ultimately God's larger Purpose and Plan for our lives.

It might be interesting to note here that two of the most prominent people in the New Testament received NO answers to their prayers. These two people both prayed to God three times with fervent requests, and their requests were not answered in the way they wanted. One person was God's own Son, Jesus, who prayed three times in the Garden of Gethsemane saying:

"Father, if it is Your will, take this cup away from Me; nevertheless not My will, but Yours, be done." *(Luke 22:42).* We know that the "cup" to which Jesus was referring was the suffering and separation that he was about to endure as he was headed to the cross. Jesus did not receive a verbal NO answer, but the fact that the cup **did not** pass from Him was an implication that the answer was NO. The fact that God's will was done in and through His son to accomplish His larger purpose and plan of salvation for the world lets us know that God did not grant His son's request.

As we look back at our text for this message, Paul is the other person who prayed three times and to whom it would seem was given a NO answer—not because of anything He had done wrong, but to **keep Him from doing wrong**, to keep him from becoming prideful. Paul said: "… Lest I should be exalted above measure by the abundance of the revelations, a thorn in the flesh was given to me, a messenger of Satan to buffet me, lest I be exalted above measure."*(2 Corinthians 12:7)* As we note the context of the text, we see that Paul had been caught up to the third heaven and had been given some great revelations to undergird him for his mission to the Gentiles. But to keep Paul from becoming arrogant and conceited about these revelations he had received; God had allowed Satan to torment him with some hardship or disability.

Students of the Bible know that there's been much speculation and discussion among Bible commentators concerning the identity of this "thorn." We really don't know what Paul's thorn in the flesh was because he doesn't tell us. Some have suggested that it was malaria, epilepsy, or a disease of the eyes. Whatever the case, it was a chronic and debilitating problem, which at times kept him from his work. This thorn was a hindrance to his ministry, and he prayed for its removal; but God refused.[40] And because we don't know what the thorn was, I dare not try to give you any insights or any "thorn theology." Along with keeping Paul from becoming "exalted above measure" about what he had seen and heard, God withheld the removal of the thorn to show Paul that by grace, he could live with the thorn; he could live with his problem, whatever it was. He said to Paul: "…My grace is sufficient for you, for My strength is made perfect in weakness." *(2 Corinthians 12:9)*

We could speculate all the day long, but because God's ways are not our ways, and God's thoughts are not our thoughts, we will never fully understand the "why" of God's answers and His actions, for God moves in mysterious ways, His wonders to perform, and we must learn to accept His mysterious ways. Unfortunately, some of us are just like children, and we only accept what's nice and comfortable, and we tend to reject the not so nice and the not so comfortable. Readily and without question, we accept YES answers when it's in answer to what we want. When we ourselves or even a loved one has been healed of an illness, and that healing has come about according to ours and the doctor's plan and time frame, we take that as a YES answer, and we're glad about it. When we got the job or the promotion that we wanted, and it happened according to our plan and our timetable, we take that as a YES answer and we're glad about it. When somehow, miraculously, that pesky co-worker was transferred to another department, out of our space and out of our sight, we take that as a YES answer to a desperate prayer that we prayed, and we're glad about it. When we finally opened the door one day and our prodigal child returned and said: "Mom, Dad, I'm home," we take that as a YES answer to a long time prayer that we've been praying, and we're happy about it. We take these as YES answers, give God praise, and all is right with the world.

On the other hand, we tend to have a little problem when the answer is WAIT because some of us are impatient, and we want what we want when we want it, and we sometimes want to treat God like a Cosmic Bellboy to whom we want to snap our fingers and have God snap to attention and do our bidding. But it doesn't work that way. Then when the answer is NO, that's a bigger problem, because again, we don't like to be refused. We don't like to be told we can't have what we want. It feels like a rejection, and some of us don't respond well to rejection.

Well, what should I do? What should I do when the answer is NO? How do I respond when the answer is WAIT? How do I accept the answer when it's not what I was hoping for? (I'm glad you asked).

First, when we don't get the answer we wanted, we must **Acknowledge God's Omniscience**—*the fact that He knows EVERYTHING*. In other words, God knows all about our situation, and that He knows what's best in our situation. The Bible is not explicit on this point, but it is implied that Paul acknowledged God's omniscience; that Paul acknowledged that God knew about his problem. Paul prayed to God three times concerning his problem and this is an indication that he must have believed that God knew all about his "thorn," and he believed that God was able to do something about the thorn. Therefore, we must also believe that God knows what's going on with us. The Bible says that "…He who comes to God must believe that He is, and that He is a rewarder of those who diligently seek Him" (*Hebrews 11:6*). We must believe that God knows the specific problem; that He knows how long we've had the problem; that He knows how the problem is affecting us; and that He knows what to do about it. Yes, right now, our problem may be causing us a bit of suffering. We might be in pain; we might be in some distress. Some of us might even be at the point of giving up, but just hold on and hold out a little while longer and remember and believe that **God Knows all about it!** We have not been promised to always be given YES answers, but God has not forgotten about us, and He has promised never to leave us nor forsake us. The songwriter said it this way…… *"Though the load gets heavy sometimes, we're never left alone to bear it all. Just ask for strength and keep on toiling, though the teardrops fall. We have the joy of this assurance, our Heavenly Father will always answer prayer—(maybe not the way we want Him to, or at the time we want Him to, but nevertheless, He will answer prayer) for He knows, oh yes He knows, just how much we can bear."*[41]

Not only must we acknowledge God's omniscience, but we must also **acknowledge God's Omnipotence**—acknowledge that God has the **power** to take care of our situation according to His will. In praying to God three times about the thorn, Paul believed that God did indeed have the power to remove the thorn. Regardless of what our situation may be, there is nothing too hard for God and He has the power to rectify the situation. He has the power to resolve the issue. He has the power to "remove the thorn," and to do it to our satisfaction if that is His will. On the other hand, to solve the problem to our satisfaction may not be His will. It might be His will to let the problem stay with us and, by His power, to help us to deal with it. Whatever His will, when the answer is NO, we need to acknowledge that He has all knowledge and all power, and above all, we must remember that God is sovereign, and He can and will do whatever He wants to do when He wants to do it.

Not only must we acknowledge God's omniscience and His omnipotence, **but secondly**, when we don't get the answer that we're looking for, we must **Accept God's answer and Accept God's Grace.** We know that Paul did not receive a specific "No, Paul, I will not remove the thorn." But the fact that the "thorn" was not removed is an implied NO response, and apparently, Paul accepted this answer graciously. However, the Bible leaves me curious about a couple of things concerning this part of the text (and perhaps you may be curious also). The Bible reports that Paul prayed and pleaded with the Lord three times to have the thorn removed. Now I wondered, first, how long was it between Paul's prayers? Did Paul pray three times in one day at different intervals? Did he pray once every morning for three days? Or was it perhaps once a week for three weeks or longer? And I also wonder if Paul received any kind of answer the first two times, or was there only silence until the third time? And if there was silence the first two times, what was Paul's reaction to the silence? (Just some questions that I had as I studied this text). And since the Bible is silent on these issues of mine concerning Paul, and since God has been silent about giving me an answer, I can only speculate considering my own experiences. I've prayed many prayers, some prayers repeatedly, and it seemed that God was silent. It seemed that I was not getting an answer, and sometimes I wondered if God even heard me, so I prayed again. And even now, there are some prayers that I've sent up on the figurative express elevator, and apparently the answer is WAIT because the elevator has not returned and is probably taking the local route. I think somebody can identify with me. You've been praying for a loved one's salvation. You've been praying for a child or a grandchild to give his or her life to Christ. You've been praying for healing for someone. You've been praying for a job opportunity to open. You've been praying for a wayward child to come back home. Ladies, you've been praying for a gentleman friend who could possibly become your spouse. Gentlemen, you've been praying for a lady friend who could possibly become your spouse. You've been praying for a "thorn" (some illness, some condition, some situation) to be removed, and yet, it has not happened. How are you accepting this? How are you handling this? How are you dealing with the answers of NO, WAIT, or perhaps even more troubling, how are you dealing with the silence on the subject?

When Paul received his answer, it wasn't a flat-out NO. Instead, he received God's Grace. God's words to Paul were: "…My Grace is sufficient for you, for my strength is made perfect in weakness." (*2 Corinthians 12:9*) What is grace? Grace is God's unmerited favor, something that can't be earned; something that can't be bought; something that can't be worked for….just God, in His infinite love, wisdom, and mercy giving to us that which we really do not deserve. God gave Paul unmerited favor.

In asking God three times to remove the thorn, Paul may have felt determined and entitled to be delivered from that thorn—that he had a right to be healed. After all, wasn't he doing everything he could to be all that God wanted him to be? Wasn't he traveling near and far, spreading the Word, making disciples, and planting churches? Didn't he have the right to be unencumbered by some disability that could hamper his progress? We think like that sometimes, don't we? When we're doing all that we can to be that all that God would have us to be, we think we have a right to be healthy and whole. It doesn't work that way, though, and instead of God giving Paul an <u>Entitlement,</u> God gave Paul an <u>Empowerment.</u> God didn't give Paul what He wanted, but He gave Paul what he needed. God gave him grace to accept the "thorn;" God gave him the power to endure the "thorn", and God gave him strength to cope with the "thorn." Depending on your perspective, that's a miracle. God looked beyond Paul's "thorn" and saw Paul's need--his need to know and understand that God's grace was greater than the "thorn." God saw Paul's need to know and understand that in his weakness, God's strength would suffice and sustain him. This is the lesson for us. We need to get to the place where we can wrap our minds around the biblical principle that we will not always receive YES answers to our prayers; that God will not always perform a miracle for us in the way that we're expecting; that He will not always remove a pain, a problem, or perhaps even a person who seems to be a "thorn" in our flesh, but He will give us the grace to accept, the power to endure, and, the strength to cope. When we are weak, if we allow God to fill us with His power and His strength, then we are stronger than we could ever be on our own. And in our weakness, His strength will carry us; in our weakness, His strength will undergird us; in our weakness, His strength will support us; in our weakness, His strength will strengthen us and we'll be able to do what God would have us do…in spite of our pains, problems or persecutions.

Finally, when we don't get the answer that we're looking for, we must continue to **Abide in Him and to Affirm His Lordship over our lives**. Too often, when the answer is NO, we get angry with God and we turn away from Him. We stay away from church; we turn away from His Word; we turn away from prayer, and we turn away from praise. We whine and cry and complain. And then if we do come to church, we're feeling so bad, and so sad, and sometimes so mad, we fold our arms and sit down on Him and withhold our praise and our worship of Him. Sometimes, just like little children, we pout and sulk because we can't have our way. But in those times when the answer is NO or WAIT, we really need to get a grip and get over ourselves. We need to stop whining and complaining, get it together, accept the NO answer and the WAIT answer with grace, continue to abide in Him and let His word abide in us (*John 15:7 paraphrased),* and continue to recognize Him as Lord and Master of our lives. Although it may seem to be a difficult task, believe it or not, it can be done. When the answer is NO, it doesn't make God any less God nor does it make God any less good. He's still our Father; He's still the only One Who can do for us what no other power can do; He's still the one who can do exceeding abundantly above all that we ask or think (*Ephesians 3:20-paraphrased);* He's still the Great "I AM"*(Exodus 3:14)*—the one who is able to heal, set free and deliver. He's still Jehovah Jireh – our provider (*Genesis 22:14*); He's still Jehovah-Shalom – our peace (*Judges 6:24*). He's still Jehovah-Shammah – the One who is there (*Ezekiel 48:35*), and just as God looks beyond our faults and sees our need, by faith, we need to look beyond the NO answer and the WAIT answer and see that "…all things are working together for our good…" *(Romans 8:28 - paraphrased).* By faith, we need to look beyond what feels like a rejection and try to understand the response considering the sovereignty of God.

When God said to Paul, "My grace is sufficient for you, for my strength is made perfect in weakness,"*(2 Corinthians 12:9)* Paul's response was: "Therefore, most gladly, I will rather boast in my infirmities that the power of Christ may rest upon me" *(2 Corinthians 12:9)*. Paul got it!! He understood it!! He understood that in his weakness, God's strength was <u>all</u> he needed. Whatever that "thorn" was, whatever problems it was causing him, Paul understood that he could admit and acknowledge his problem, and at the same time abide in Christ and affirm Christ's Lordship in his life so that he could continue to receive His blessings. Paul said: "...I take pleasure in infirmities, in reproaches, in needs, in persecutions, in distresses, for Christ's sake. For when I am weak, then I am strong" (*2 Corinthians 12:10*). Paul understood and he could "...count it all joy" (*James 1:2 paraphrased*) because He knew that God's grace was sufficient; that God's strength would make him strong; that God's power would pull him through. And that's the miracle—when we can understand, accept, abide, and affirm the Lordship of Christ despite the NO or WAIT answers to our request.

Now I know that you might find Paul's response a difficult concept, and you may be asking the questions: How can I boast about anything when I'm so burdened down? How can I take pleasure in my problem when my problem is causing me so much pain? How can I feel good when I feel so bad? How can I be happy when I'm hurting? How can I sing when I am suffering? How can I be loving when I've been left alone and lonely? How can I rise above the "thorn" in my flesh that's tormenting me? My response would be: Don't be fooled by the enemy into thinking that a WAIT answer is FINAL, or that a NO answer is FATAL. "Do not be conformed to this world, but be transformed by the renewing of you mind..." (*Romans 12:2*), and "...let this mind be in you which was also in Christ Jesus..." (*Philippians 2:5*). Be assured that You **can** accept God's answer, and by His grace, you **can** "do all things through Christ who strengthens you" (*Philippians 4:13 – paraphrased*). Don't let a NO answer be a negative but see it as a positive. Don't let a NO answer be a stumbling block, but let it be a steppingstone to a new perspective. Don't let a NO answer cause you to sin in word or deed, but rather let it become an affirmation of your faith. Despite the NO and the "thorn," "press toward the goal for the prize of the upward call of God in Christ Jesus" (*Philippians 3:14*). Paul had a "thorn in the flesh." I'm saying to you don't let a NO answer become a "thorn" in your flesh. Don't let that NO become something that irritates you and nags at you and agitates you, and bothers you to no end, but rather, recognize that a NO answer now might be a blessing in disguise. A NO answer now may be making room for a YES answer later. A NO answer to you now might be a YES answer for a loved one now. A NO now might be keeping you from an unseen danger down the line. Don't turn your back on God! In spite of the NO, in spite of the "thorn," go on and raise a praise and "...bless the Lord at all times and let His praise continually be in your mouth" *(Psalm 34:1 - paraphrased).* Despite the NO, despite the "thorn," choose to worship and "make a joyful shout to the Lord and serve Him with gladness" *(Psalm 100:1,2 - paraphrased).* Despite the NO, despite the "thorn," remember that "God is still your refuge and your strength, a very present help in the time of trouble." *(Psalm 46:1 - paraphrased).* Despite the NO, realize that there are things in life we don't understand, but God is still in control and He has a divine plan for our lives. The NO answers, the YES answers, the WAIT answers—they "all work together for good to those who love God, to those who are called according to His purpose." *(Romans 8:28)*

ENDNOTES

1   http://www.dictionary.com.
2   Bell and Daldy. The Rector and his Friends: Dialogues on Some of the Leading Religious Questions of the Day. <u>Miracles and Special Providences</u>. York Street. Covent Garden. 1869. pg. 162.
3   ibid.
4   http://www.dictionary.com
5   Bell and Daldy. The Rector and his Friends: Dialogues on Some of the Leading Religious Questions of the Day. <u>Miracles and Special Providences</u>. York Street. Covent Garden. 1869. pg. 162
6   https://genius.com/Stuart-hamblen-its-no-secret-lyrics.
7   https://www.gotquestions.org/Jesus-Mary-woman.html
8   https://secondhandsongs.com/work/170115/all Dorothy Love Coates.
9   http://www.dictionary.com
10 https://hymnary.org/text/hark_tis_the_shepherds_voice_i_hear
11 Life Application Bible Commentary. Tyndale Publishers. Carol Stream 2019. pgs. 2161, 2162.
12 http://www.dictionary.com.
13 New National Baptist Hymnal. <u>"Because He Lives."</u> Bill and Gloria Gaither. National Baptist Publishing Board. Nashville.1979. pg. 106.
14 New National Baptist Hymnal. <u>"We'll Understand it Better By and By"</u>. C.A. Tindley/F.A. Clark. National Baptist Publishing Board. Nashville. 1979. pg. 325.
15 New National Baptist Hymnal. <u>"My Father Watches Over Me."</u> Rev. C.W. Martin/Chas.H. Gabriel. National Baptist Publishing Board. Nashville. 1979. pg. 214.
16 New National Baptist Hymnal. <u>"Yield Not to Temptation."</u> Horatio R. Palmer. National Baptist Publishing Board. Nashville. 1979. pg. 188.
17 https://genius.com/Dorothy-norwood-victory-is-mine-lyrics.
18 https://genius.com/The-brooklyn-tabernacle-choir-so-you-would-know-lyrics
19 https://genius.com/Andrae-crouch-let-the-church-say-amen-lyrics
20 ibid.
21 https://www.elyrics.net/read/m/milton-brunson-lyrics/i_m-free-lyrics.html

22 https://www.lyrics.com/track/2652431/Gaither+Vocal+Band/He+Touched+Me.

23 Life Application Bible Commentary. Tyndale Publishers. Carol Stream 2019. pg. 769.

24 New National Baptist Hymnal. "God Will Take Care of You." Civilla D. Martin. National Baptist Publishing Board. Nashville. 1979. pg. 220.

25 https://www.biblegateway.com/resources/all-women-bible/Woman-Issue-Blood

26 ibid

27 https://hymnary.org/text/father_i_stretch_my_hands_to_thee. Charles Wesley.

28 New National Baptist Hymnal. "Something Within." L.E. Campbell. National Baptist Publishing Board. Nashville. 1979. pg. 275.

29 https://www.studylight.org/commentaries/dsb/matthew-8.html. WilliamBarclay.

30 https://hymnary.org/text/sometimes_i_feel_discouraged_spiritual. There is a Balm in Gilead.

31 https://www.lyrics.com/track/2652431/Gaither+Vocal+Band/He+Touched+Me

32 New National Baptist Hymnal. "Just a Little Talk With Jesus." Cleavant Derricks. National Baptist Publishing Board. Nashville. 1979. pg. 298.

33 https://genius.com/Stuart-hamblen-its-no-secret-lyrics

34 New National Baptist Hymnal. "Just a Little Talk With Jesus." Cleavant Derricks. National Baptist Publishing Board. Nashville. 1979. pg. 298.

35 Life Application Bible Commentary. Tyndale Publishers. Carol Stream.2019. pg. 2282.

36 Life Application Bible Commentary. Tyndale Publishers. Carol Stream.2019. pg. 2305.

37 New National Baptist Hymnal. "I Heard The Voice of Jesus Say." Horatius Bonar. National Baptist Publishing Board. Nashville. 1979. pg. 310.

38 New National Baptist Hymnal. "Saved, Saved!. Jack P. Schofield. National Baptist Publishing Board. Nashville. 1979. pg. 139.

39 New National Baptist Hymnal. "Thank You, Lord." Seth Sykes and Beth Sykes. National Baptist Publishing Board. Nashville. 1979. pg. 464.

40 Life Application Bible Commentary. Tyndale Publishers. Carol Stream.2019. pg. 2655.

41 New National Baptist Hymnal. "He Knows Just How Much You Can Bear." Roberta Martin. National Baptist Publishing Board. Nashville. 1979. pg. 250.

Printed in the United States
By Bookmasters